The Vitiligo Diet (CookBook)

A Nutritional Approach To Curing Vitiligo

TABLE OF CONTENTS

INTRODUCTION

As the medical world is now realizing, the majority of chronic conditions, including vitiligo, are linked with inflammation within the body. Basically, modern diets are conducive towards an inflammatory state, and this is resulting in rapidly increasing rates of ailments and diseases. Inflammation is how your body responds to something painful, irritating or, even potentially, harmful. Having abnormal levels of inflammation in your body can put you at an increased risk for developing heart disease, cancer, and other life-threatening conditions.

In vitiligo, the melanocytes (pigment-producing cells) are NOT dead, but simply non-functional. I like to compare it to type 2 diabetes, where the pancreas is still producing insulin, however, this insulin does not work very well. The level of inflammation within your body largely dictates how well your organs work and how healthy you are. Of course, it is not the whole picture and there are some other factors (e.g. genetics) that we have no control on. However, diet is the major modifiable factor and it is crucial if you want to get rid of your vitiligo. The key is adopting an anti-inflammatory diet.

Anti-inflammatory lifestyle diets have been recommended by health care professionals for decades due to the health benefits derived from the diet, however, it is suggested that 7 out of 10 adults have never even heard of the diet! This is largely because of the lack of available information about the diet. Go to your local library or book store and you will be fortunate to find even one or two books on anti-inflammatory eating. Most who have heard of the diet only have their physicians' advice or the internet to gain information on the diet. The benefits obtained through following an anti-inflammatory diet are so valuable that word of the diet needs to begin to spread like wildfire.

Though scientific data on the benefits of the anti-inflammatory diet continues to be researched, experts have concluded that the main advantages of the lifestyle diet which have been proven to date include:

- ✓ Decreases risk of heart disease
- ✓ Decreases risk of diabetes
- ✓ Reduces blood triglycerides and blood pressure
- ✓ Helps to maintain and control existing cardiac problems
- ✓ Helps reduce painful arthritis flare-ups
- ✓ Relieves tender and/or stiff joints
- ✓ Discontinuance of many over-the-counter/prescription medications

Inflammation is a condition within our bodies which can trigger a wide array of chronic diseases. It is not bias, it can happen to anyone, woman or man; child or adult. If you take away the chance for inflammation, you will reduce the risk of various diseases and disorders. Constant, frequently reoccurring, or even just occasional inflammation can lead to more than just ill physical health. The pain and various side effects associated with inflammation can also lead to depression, anxiety, and other mental/emotional disorders. This is above and beyond the benefits it has for curing your vitiligo.

An anti-vitiligo/anti-inflammatory diet consists of foods that are proven to prevent, control, or reduce the level of inflammation in one's body; thereby being conducive to restoring the melanocytes' optimal function.

Some foods are more powerful in the reduction of inflammation then others while there are also foods that will increase inflammation. Knowing which foods are which will make this an easy diet to follow – there is no need for counting calories, carbohydrates, etc. There is not any strict portion control. There are no food logs to keep up with; no medications; no crazy hoops to jump through; no inconvenient schedule to keep. All this lifestyle diet consists of is making sure you are eating more of certain foods, while limiting or completely avoiding other foods. This will, without a doubt, be one of the easiest diets you have ever followed. This, in turn, ensures that you will be more likely to stick with it and be successful at it. You can do your part to protect yourself and your loved ones by preparing meals and snacks using foods that will help combat inflammation, cure vitiligo and also prevent it from happening in those who do not have it yet. This also doesn't mean spending hours slaving away in the kitchen making everything from scratch. Toss your kid an apple – there you go! There are so many foods which will help to prevent, control, and reduce inflammation that you can keep your pantry and refrigerator stocked with. There are simple meals and snacks which you can make in a matter of minutes with very little fuss or concentration. On the opposite side of the coin, there are also foods that can trigger or increase the levels of inflammation in one's body and can cause or aggravate your vitiligo. Once you know which these foods are you can avoid them at all costs (or at the very least, greatly limit consumption).

Throughout this book you will learn the benefits behind consuming an anti-vitiligo & anti-inflammatory diet. You will begin to understand the factors which make up this diet and how these factors can affect the level of inflammation in a person's body. Finally you will find 150 recipes to help get you started in four main categories, including:

- ✓ Breakfast Recipes
- ✓ Lunch Recipes
- ✓ Dinner Recipes
- ✓ Snack Recipes

The ultimate goal of this cookbook is to help open the door to an anti-inflammatory diet lifestyle. It is for all individuals, so that they may find optimum health and well-being. You do not need to have problems with inflammation to participate in this diet nor does this diet need to be recommended by a doctor (although, it is always a good idea to consult with your physician before beginning any new diet regimen). There are no special packaged foods, bars, or drinks, no gimmicks. All that is required of you is that you stick mostly to the foods on the approved list and, as much as possible, steer clear of the high-risk foods. That's it – that's all there really is to it. The anti-inflammatory diet is one that can easily be adjusted around you and/or your family's busy schedule. With the anti-inflammatory diet, you can enjoy how great you feel and it will boost the healing process from vitiligo.

PART ONE

What is an Anti-Vitiligo/Anti-Inflammation Diet?

1

The Build-Up to an Anti-Vitiligo/ Anti-Inflammatory Diet

Before beginning a new diet, especially one that the whole family could possibly be participating in, it is vital that you pick the diet apart from the inside out. What is it? What are the benefits of it? Which types of foods will I be encouraged/discouraged to eat? How difficult is the diet? How much time/effort must be dedicated to the diet each week? Will I have to take any supplements or other medications? What hoops will I have to jump through in order to be successful at this diet? Is it safe for me? Is it safe for my family? The possible questions are endless.

The anti-vitiligo/ anti-inflammatory diet is simple. There are really only a few main components to this lifestyle diet. Consider these to be the Golden Rules of the Anti-Vitiligo/Anti-Inflammatory Diet. If you stick with these "rules" then you can't go wrong.

The Golden Rules of an Anti-Vitiligo/ Anti-Inflammatory Diet

There are several "rules" surrounding the anti-inflammatory lifestyle diet. By abiding by these rules, you will find it that much easier to understand and maintain the diet. These rules are as follows:

1. Eat a balanced diet full of a variety of whole, healthy foods.
2. Consume ONLY "good" healthy fats – Unsaturated Fats.
3. Eat plenty of fruits and vegetables.
4. Consume at least ONE source of omega-3 fatty acids each and every day.
5. Eat a diet high in protein from lean sources, such as lean-choice meats.
6. Consume whole grains daily.
7. Drink plenty of water.
8. Minimize your consumption of processed and refined foods.

In addition, it is crucial that you avoid blueberries at all costs as these contain a substance that blocks the production of melanin (pigment).

Let's go over a few of these "rules" in further detail, shall we?

Incorporate Healthy Fats:

It is so important to understand the difference between healthy fats and unhealthy fats. You need a regular consumption of healthy fats in your diet. Each of the different types of fat play a role in how properly your body functions – whether it be positive or negative roles. However, so many people think of fat as just that – fat. They view it as a negative and try to stay away from fat altogether, thinking that by steering clear of all fat that they are actually doing their bodies good, when in fact, they are really only hurting more than helping themselves. Let's take a look at the different types of fats and what rolw they play in your diet and overall well-being.

First, let's go over the different types of fats - the "Good" and the "Bad" fats – and the types of food sources that they are commonly found in:

TYPES OF FATS			
"GOOD" FATS		"BAD" FATS	
Monounsaturated	Polyunsaturated	Saturated	Trans
Olive Oil	Vegetable Oil	Whole Milk	Most Margerines
Peanut Oil	Corn Oil	Red Meat	Baked Goods
			Many Processed Foods
Canola Oil	Soybean Oil	Butter	Fast Foods
Avocados	Safflower Oil	Cheese	Many Snack Foods
Almonds	Cottonseed Oil	Coconut Oil	Vegetable Shortenings
	Fish		Partially Hydrogenated Vegetable Oils.

"Good Fat": Monounsaturated Fats

Monounsaturated Fats are fats that are found in olive and canola oils, avocados, etc. and have proven over time to have protective properties over our health. They are known to reduce/prevent heart disease, reducing cholesterol, digestive health, brain health, and so on.

When it comes to an anti-inflammatory diet, olive oil is a secret weapon often brought to the table as it loaded with antioxidants. There is a compound in olive oil called Oleocanthal which has shown to fight inflammation as well as, if not better, than nonsteroidal anti-inflammatory drugs, such as Ibuprofen.

"Good Fat": Polyunsaturated Fats

When it comes to Polyunsaturated Fats, there are two main types:

1. Omega-3 Fats

2. Omega-6 Fats

Both types of Omega are essential fatty acids which are vital for optimum health. However, the human body does not naturally produce either Omega on its own, so it is up to us to supply our bodies with it from external sources, such as through diet or supplements.

Research shows that Omega-3's help to reduce or prevent the level of inflammation in the body. Doctors have been prescribing Omega-3 supplements to patients with arthritis or those who are at high risk for diseases, such as heart disease and certain types of cancer, such as breast, prostate, and colon cancers. In addition to reducing inflammation and reducing the risk of heart disease and cancer, Omega-3 also helps prevent or control symptoms of:

- Diabetes
- High Cholesterol
- High Blood Pressure
- Lupus
- Osteoporosis
- Depression
- Alzheimer's and other memory disorders
- Psychiatric disorders such as Bipolar Disorder, Schizophrenia, and Attention Deficit/Hyperactivity Disorder (ADHD)
- Skin Disorders
- Macular Degeneration
- Inflammatory Bowel Disease (IBD)
- Asthma
- Menstrual Pain or Disorders

If you don't like taking supplements, you can get the same results through eating a regular intake of fatty fish, such as salmon, halibut, and so on. A regular consumption of Omega-3 is safe for children and adults of all ages. For a steady intake of Omega-3's, consume the following on a weekly basis:

- Eat at least 2 (4-ounce) servings of fatty fish per week, OR
- Take DAILY: 1 Omega-3 Fish Oil supplement which has 1g. combined EPA & DHA.

Note concerning Omega-6 Fats: When maintaining an anti-inflammatory diet, it is important to maintain a reduced intake of Omega-6 fats as they are known to actually increase inflammation levels where as Omega-3 fats are known to decrease inflammation. When you eat foods or take supplements rich in Omega-3, the Omega-3 fuels the production of two types of acid known as eicosapentaenoic acid and docosahexaenoic acid, these acids working together create anti-inflammatory componenets referred to as Prostaglandins and Leukotrienes.

What many anti-inflammatory dieters do is however much they do not consume in

Omega-6, they will add that missed amount in Omega-3. This means they are receiving the full amount of fatty acids their bodies need per week, they are just shifting the weight more towards Omega-3. This does wonders in reducing the amount of inflammation in their bodies. The correct Omega-3 to Omega-6 weekly ratio should be between 2:1 and 4:1 servings per week and to help you get started, the recipes listed in this book are ones that help you consume more Omega-3 while decreasing Omega-6.

Before you take on grocery shopping for your anti-inflammatory diet, familiarize yourself with which food sources are rich in both types of Omega. For instance, Omega-6 fatty acids are found in sources such as:

- Processed Foods/Prepackaged Foods/Foods with a long shelf life, such as Hostess Twinkies which reportedly have a shelf life of nearly forever!
- Safflower, Corn, Sunflower, Sesame, Cottonseed, Peanut Oils
- Most Margarines

Therefore, while grocery shopping for an anti-inflammatory lifestyle diet; it is wise to minimalize the purchase of these types of foods. Now, many people wonder, "If I need to reduce how much Omega-6 fatty acids I consume, why is Omega-6 not considered a "bad" fat?" Omega-6 fatty acids are absolutely "good" fats, however, for a person prone to flare-ups of inflammation, it is best if they monitor the amount of Omega-6 they are ingesting ONLY because of Omega-6's tendency to increase inflammation. This by no means suggests that Omega-6 fatty acids are bad for your health, it only advises that because Omega-6 has been shown to promote inflammation that those who follow an anti-inflammatory diet watch the amount of Omega-6 that they are consuming.

"Bad Fat": Saturated Fats

Saturated fats are considered bad fats because they have a reputation of causing heart disease and stroke due to the role they play in increasing levels of LDL (bad cholesterol) and decreasing HDL (good cholesterol). Food sources which are main carriers of saturated fats include some meats, dairy products made from whole-milk, coconut/palm oils, etc.

Saturated fats should be used only in limited moderation or a daily allowance of no more than 10% saturated fat. Saturated fats are also culprits in raising inflammation levels as they are known to change the makeup of what would otherwise be harmless bacteria in the gut and makes that would-be-harmless bacteria harmful as the change in composition triggers an immune reaction which causes increases in inflammation, pain, and tissue damage. Saturated fats decrease the fluidity of the cell membranes, and in turn disrupt the functioning of their receptors and ion channels. This results in deranged cell function. This is exactly the reason why, for example, a diet high in saturated fats causes diabetes - because the cells stop being responsive to insulin. In the case of vitiligo, the cells stop secreting melanin.

"Bad Fat": Trans Fats

Trans fats were invented long ago as a way to prolong the shelf life of polyunsaturated fats by infusing the food sources with hydrogen gas in order to partially hydrogenate the foods to make them last longer. They did this after it was determined that saturated fats led to heart disease/strokes and they realized that polyunsaturated fats were actually healthier than saturated fats – the problem? Many of the food sources containing polyunsaturated fats spoiled too quickly. Through this "manipulation" of polyunsaturated fats, partially hydrogenated vegetable oils, such as cottonseed, soybean, corn oils, etc. were created. What's ironic is that scientists invented trans-polyunsaturated fats in order to sway people away from saturated fats because of the high-risk saturated fats played in heart disease and stroke but when in the end, when all was said and done, these scientists did nothing more than introduce people to ADDITIONAL food sources which could *also* lead to heart disease and strokes, thus, placing trans fats on the "bad" fats list right alongside saturated fats.

The moral of the story – trans fats are bad for your health, regardless of if they were originally derived from polyunsaturated fats. Trans fats are mainly found in packaged and processed foods, such as baked goods, packaged snack foods, etc. The consumption of trans fats should absolutely be minimalized, particularly for those following an anti-inflammatory lifestyle diet because with the consumption of trans fat comes an increase in omega-6, which as stated earlier, contains components that increase levels of inflammation.

Eat a balanced diet full of a variety of whole, healthy foods.

How does eating a whole foods diet affect one's battle with vitiligo, you ask? Well, it's simple, really. Eating a balanced diet of whole foods is vital, not only for getting rid of vitiligo, but also for overall optimum health is because a diet comprised of whole foods – fresh fruits and vegetables, lean meats and fish, low-fat dairy products, and whole grains – is a diet that is power-packed with vitamins, nutrients, and disease-fighting antioxidants.

There are several reasons as to why a whole foods diet is an ideal component of the anti-vitiligo/ anti-inflammatory lifestyle, for instance, a whole foods diet steers clear of processed and refined foods, which in turn helps lead to decreased inflammation and optimise the melanocytes' function. Furthermore, a whole foods diet, along with regular physical activity, promotes weight loss and helps one meet and maintain their ideal weight. A whole foods diet can help prevent obesity, which in turn leads to decreased inflammation and better functioning of the pigment-producing cells. The list goes on and on. Let's look at the main components of the anti-inflammatory diet.

Caloric Intake on the Anti-Vitiligo/ Anti-Inflammatory Diet

The proper amount of calories is an important factor in any diet and every diet has different "caloric rules." For instance, if your main dieting goal is to lose weight, then your daily amount of allowed calories would be very restrictive. What is the main component to losing weight? The answer: you have to burn more calories than you consume. Let's say you are on a 1500 calorie a day diet to lose weight. In order to ensure weight loss you had better be burning at least 1600 calories per day, but realistically, you should be burning closer to 2000 calories per day. If you consume 1500 calories per day and you burn off 1500 calories per day, then you are not losing weight, but you are merely maintaining your current weight.

With weight loss diets often comes extreme calorie counting and who wants to have to take on that responsibility on top of an already hectic life? Thankfully, with the anti-inflammatory diet you will not have to log every single calorie consumed each day – unless, of course, you opt to do so!
When it comes to calories and the anti-inflammatory diet, try to follow the following guidelines:

- Most adults, both men and women, who are moderately to highly active, need to consume between 2,000 and 3,000 calories per day.
- For women, or those individuals who participate in little to no daily physical activity need fewer calories whereas men or those who participate in a moderate to high daily activity level.
- The best way that daily calories should be distributed in a anti-inflammatory diet are as follows:
  - → 30% of calories should come from fat.
  - → 20% - 30% of calories should come from protein.
  - → 40% - 50% of calories should come from carbohydrates.
- Always try to include at least one fat source, one carbohydrate source, and one protein source at each meal.

Carbohydrate Intake on the Anti-Vitiligo/ Anti-Inflammatory Diet

Ahhh, carbs... they are quite the challenge. So many carb-rich food sources are so delicious that it can be very easy to eat more carbs than we should be eating each day. Then there's the confusion over which carbs are "good" carbs and which are to be considered "bad" carbs. Your body needs carbohydrates even more than it needs fats and proteins in order for it to function properly, however, it needs the *right* type of carbs.

You should not be afraid of carbs. You need carbs. Some of the most nutrient and antioxidant-rich foods are high in carbohydrates. However, when following an anti-inflammatory diet, it is important to decipher the good from the bad when it comes to carbs – just like fats, some carbs prevent/alleviate inflammation while others trigger it. "Bad" carbs include carbs that are high in sugar and processed/refined foods: white rice, most packaged cereals, most breads/bagels, white flour, granulated sugar, etc. The reason "bad" carbs promote inflammation is really sort of two-part:

1. "Bad" carbs are void of fiber, which means that they are very hard for the body to digest.
2. "Bad" carbs are extremely easy to eat too much of, there for, there is an overabundance of "bad" carbs that your body will have a very difficult time to digest.

Because your body has a hard time to digest this overabundance of "bad" carbs, the carbs sit there in your body, unable to be burnt off or digested until they are converted into a dangerous type of saturated fats called palmitic acid which has been known to increase cholesterol and lead to heart disease and stroke. In addition to this, overeating "bad" carbs can easily lead to obesity and excess body fat which can and will cause increased levels of inflammation in the body.

When it comes to calories and the anti-inflammatory diet, try to follow the following guidelines:

- Based on a 2,000 calorie per day diet, adults should eat the following consumption og "good" carbs each day:
  - → **Men:** 240 – 300 grams of carbohydrates per day;
  - → **Women:** 160 – 200 grams of carbohydrates per day
- Most of the carbs you do consume each day should come from unprocessed/unrefined foods.
- Watch your intake of wheat flour/sugars as breads, cakes, cookies, packaged snacks, chips, etc.
- Avoid all products made using high fructose corn syrup.
- Eat sources of "good carbs" such as fruits and vegetables, whole-wheat pastas (in moderation), beans, sweet potatoes, brown rice, winter squashes, etc.

Fat Intake on the Anti-Vitiligo/ Anti-Inflammatory Diet

We have pretty much already covered the role of fats (the "good" and the "bad") in the anti-inflammatory diet, but here are a few guidelines to help ensure that you stick mainly to the "good" fats:

- Based on a 2,000 calorie-per-day diet, the recommended amount of calories coming from fats alone should not total more than 600 calories, which equals about 66-67 grams.
- When following recipes, substitute vegetable-based oils/partially-hydrogenated oils, margarines/shortenings for healthier choices of ingredients.
- Reduce how much saturated fat you consume by reducing the amount of creams, butter, high-fat dairy products, fatty meats, etc.
- Use extra-virgin olive oil as your main cooking oil of choice. This alone will cut your intake of saturated fats significantly.

- Fill your diet with "good" fats such as avocados, nuts, salmon and other fatty fish (for omega-3), nut butters, low-fat dairy products, etc.

Protein Intake on the Anti-Vitiligo/ Anti-Inflammatory Diet

Protein is an important component to a healthy diet, particularly, and anti-inflammatory diet. Allowing your body the proper amount of lean protein each day is essential for optimum health. Protein helps fight inflammation in a round-about way. An adequate amount of lean protein helps to strengthen the body's defenses against infection and disease. Because protein fights off infection, it is helping to prevent inflammation from happening in the first place, therefore, in an anti-inflammatory diet, protein is just as, if not more, important as eating healthy fats or avoiding sugar. Protein is the unsung hero of the anti-inflammatory diet, because it keeps inflammation from taking up residence in our bodies to begin with. It is absolutely vital that our bodies receive enough protein each day to keep it strong, so that it can defend itself from the invasion of infection, which in turn leads to inflammation. The following guidelines will help ensure you are getting enough protein in your diet.

- Based on a 2,000 calorie-per-day diet, your total daily intake of protein should be between 80-120 grams. If the recommended daily intake is 80-120 grams, individuals with autoimmune disorders, kidney/liver problems, and/or food allergies should eat the lessor amount of protein per day, while still maintaining at least the minimum recommended daily intake based on their caloric intake.
- A suggested 4 to 6 servings of lean protein per day is typically what is needed to help prevent infection.
- Try to get most of your daily protein from vegetable protein, beans especially, help build the body's defenses against inflammation.
    - → Beans/Peas such as soybeans, sweet peas, green beans, navy/black/kidney beans, etc. are excellent sources of vegetable protein.
- Try to get most of your animal protein from fish and natural cheeses, yogurts, and milk.
    - → Any fish, particularly oily fish such as tuna, salmon, sardines, trout, etc., are ideal sources of lean animal protein. However, because of possible toxins, avoid shark, mackerel, swordfish, marlin, and kingfish.
    - → Opt for skinless white meat poultry such as chicken and turkey, instead of dark meat portions.
    - → Lean cuts of pork such as tenderloin, Canadian bacon, and loin chops are the best protein choices.
    - → Lean cuts of beef such as sirloin, round steak, cubed steak, London broil, flank steak, extra-lean ground beef, and cuts of meat with very little marbling are the best protein choices.
    - → Nitrate-free, lean deli meats such as roast beef, turkey, chicken, ham, etc. are the best protein choices.
    - → Any and all shellfish (crab, lobster, oysters, shrimp, etc.) are great sources of protein.

→ Wild game choices such as venison, elk, wild turkey, quail, etc. are excellent sources of protein.

→ Natural, low-fat dairy products such as milk (fat-free or 1%, no higher in fat than 2% - and only in moderation), mozzarella cheese, Greek yogurt, etc. are all good sources of lean animal protein.

- Try protein powders, such as whey protein, rice protein, and hemp protein powders added to smoothies and protein shakes are good choices for protein-on-the-go and meal replacements.

Fiber Intake on the Anti-Vitiligo/ Anti-Inflammatory Diet

Through years of research, scientists have concluded that fiber is a natural anti-inflammatory which can even help reverse years of damage caused from chronic inflammation. It does this by seeking out potential threats in our bodies which could lead to inflammation and stopping them before they have a chance to do their dirty work. Most people are already keen to the fact that fiber is an important part of a healthy diet, particularly for a healthy digestive system. Besides its anti-inflammatory powers, fiber also plays a big part in preventing certain cancers, heart disease, vitiligo, Type II Diabetes, and more. Fiber helps to keep our bodies functioning on a daily basis. The following guidelines will help ensure you are getting enough fiber in your diet.

- Try to aim for 40 grams of fiber in your diet daily, regardless of your total caloric intake. This may seem like a lot, but you can easily achieve this by eating foods which are naturally high in fiber such as fruit (berries are fiber-rich), vegetables (beans are great), and whole grains.
- Look at pre-packaged cereals for excellent high-fiber choices. Look at the label to make sure the cereal offers 4 to 5 grams of bran per one-ounce serving. Just watch the fat/carbs/sugar content. Regular Cheerios or Special K are excellent choices.

Sugar Intake on the Anti-Vitiligo/ Anti-Inflammatory Diet

This one is simple. Too much sugar = Increased inflammation. Consuming sugar, especially in-between meals, sends your blood sugar levels on a roller coaster ride, in order for your body to regain a proper blood sugar level, your pancreas releases insulin which in turn triggers markers which cause inflammation in your body. Sugar acts somewhat like an irritant or trigger to induce inflammatory flare-ups; it is vital that you only eat sugar in moderation, if at all. When you reduce your intake of refined sugars, you decrease the level of inflammation in your body.

When it comes to baking, sweetening your coffee or anything else you may need sugar for, opt for healthier choices. The following guidelines will help you make healthy decisions when it comes to avoiding refined sugars and maintaining your anti-inflammatory diet.

- When cooking/baking, substitute granulated sugar for coconut palm sugar, the result/taste is the same, but much healthier. The alternating substitute ratio is 1:1,

• • •

meaning the measurements are equal (for example, if the recipe calls for 1 cup granulated sugar, the substitution will equal 1 cup coconut palm sugar).

- Fruits do contain sugar, but they offer so many other benefits so the good absolutely outweighs the bad. Continue eating fruit – don't stop because you are worried the sugar content will aggravate inflammation in your body. As a matter of fact, when you feel yourself craving sugar, turn to fruit first as it is an ideal way to satisfy cravings.
- Avoid ANY food source which contains high fructose corn syrup.
- Avoid ALL artificial sweeteners! Instead, opt for healthier, natural sweeteners such as:
  - → **Stevia:** This natural sweetener is from the South American Stevia Plant and is said to be 30 times sweeter than sugar in solid (powder) form and 300 times sweeter than sugar in its liquid form. Truvia is a popular brand of stevia sweetener.
  - → **Agave Nectar:** This is a natural sweetener extraceted from the agave plant. It is sweeter than refined sugar and is available in liquid form.
  - → **Coconut Palm Sugar (or Palm Sugar):** This is a very popular choice in natural sweeteners. It is made from coconut sap and looks like cane sugar. It is very healthy and contains potassium, micronutrients, and magnesium. This is the best substitute for granulated sugar in baking. It tastes similar and the end result is similar. In using coconut palm sugar as a substitute for granulated sugar (refined sugar) the measurements are equal – for example: 1 teaspoon of granulated sugar is equal to 1 teaspoon of coconut palm sugar. This makes it a very easy to use as a healthy alternative in baking.
  - → **Maple Syrup:** This natural sweetener is collected from the sap of sugar maple trees. It comes in light, medium, and dark liquid form. Popular on pancakes, waffles, and used frequently in baking. It is also high in calcium. *Warning:* Most bottles of "maple syrup" that you find on the shelves of the grocery store are not actually 100% natural maple syrup. Even if the bottle says "maple syrup" in truth, there is probably less than 5% to 10% real maple syrup in the bottle. If you go to health food stores, you will have a much better chance of obtaining real maple syrup.
  - → **Barley Malt:** Similar in taste to honey or dark molasses, barley malt is often a natural sweetener used in smoothies and baking. It is also loaded with a variety of vitamins and minerals.
  - → **Date Sugar:** Date sugar is a natural sweetener made from dehydrated dates which are then ground up. In using date sugar as a substitute for granulated sugar (refined sugar) the measurements are equal – for example: 1 teaspoon of granulated sugar is equal to 1 teaspoon of date sugar. This makes it a very easy to use as a healthy alternative in baking. *Warning:* do not use date sugar as a sweetener in beverages and coffee as it will not dissolve in liquids. It is best to use in baking.
  - → **Fructose:** Fructose is a natural sweetener born from fruit sugars. It is twice as sweet as refined sugar, so in recipes reduce the amount of refined sugar that the recipe calls for by half. If using as a sweetener for beverages, same rule applies – if you typically sweeten your iced tea with 2 teaspoons of granulated sugar then only add in 1 teaspoon of fructose.

→ **Raw Honey:** Honey is one of the most popular choices for natural sweeteners. It has been used longer than any other natural sweetener. It is made by bees from the nectar of flowers. It is available in hundreds of different types, colors, and flavors – the flavor really depends on the type of flower blossoms the honey was born from. It is sold in a variety of ways: on the comb, as natural crystals, as a liquid, as a spreadable, whipped mixture (similar to a tub of butter), and more.

→ **Xylitol:** A natural sweetener found in berries, fruit, and a variety of vegetables. It is available mainly in crystalline form and is safe for use by diabetics.

→ **Maltose:** Born from the starch of rice and grains. The staches are cooked, fermented, and converted into sugar. Usually sold in a syrupy or crystalline form.

→ **Molasses:** Made from cane that has been crushed and squeezed. It, for the most part, has a potent scent and a buttery taste. It is power-packed with calcium, iron, and potassium.

→ **Rice Sugar:** This natural sweetener is also commonly referred to as Brown Rice Syrup. It comes from brown rice starch which has been converted into maltose. It is often used to sweeten beverages, used in cooking, and often turned into a spread for breads. It is less sweet than honey, which some prefer.

→ **Turbinado Syrup:** A.K.A "Raw Sugar" or "Sugar in the Raw." It is sold as a brown crystalline form and is made from a partially-processed sugar which contains a certain percentage of molasses. It is mainly used in baking and contains fewer calories than granulated sugar.

→ **Maple Sugar:** It is a crystalline form of maple syrup – as all of the liquid has been boiled off. It is often used in baking or to sweeten hot drinks. It is also often used in making candy. Some people prefer not to use it because it is extremely sticky and messy to work with.

→ **Sorghum Syrup:** It is similar in taste and composition to molasses. It is made through squeezing juice out of the sorghum cane. The juice is then boiled down to separate out the water content until a syrup forms. It is very close to being organic which makes it very safe to consume.

Phytonutrients Intake on the Anti-Vitiligo/ Anti-Inflammatory Diet

Fruits and veggies contain phytonutrients, which are plant-based nutrients that are said to reduce both chronic and acute inflammation. Scientists also claim that eating a variety of mushrooms and bright-colored fruits and vegetables help significantly in reducing the onset of age-related inflammatory diseases, such as arthritis, heart disease, and so on.

For alleviating painful flare-ups of inflammation, produce choices such as bananas, tomatoes, berries, spinach, kale, etc. have been shown to do the trick as well as any over-the-counter or prescription medication. Also, if you put down the pills and pick up the produce, you are also canceling out your risk for being struck by a variety of other side effects just from taking the pills in order to relieve the inflammation.

Phytonutrients and fiber working together offer double the inflammatory-fighting power! The following guidelines will help ensure you are getting enough phytonutrients in your diet.

• • •

- Eat a regular diet of fruits, vegetables, and mushrooms for a regular intake of phytonutrients.
- Choose all different colors of fruits and vegetables – each color holds different phytonutrients and health benefits. So make sure you are buying a rainbow of colored produce. For example: On any given grocery shopping trip, buy a variety of colored produce, such as bright-colored berries, dark leafy greens, orange and yellow-colored fruits and vegetables, and red, red tomatoes.
- Choose organic produce when possible. Follow The Environmental Working Group's annual "Dirty Dozen" and "Clean 15" lists. The "dirty dozen" includes 12 fruits and vegetables which contain the highest amount of pesticides. These 12 produce items should always be purchased as organic. On the other hand, the "clean 15" include the top 15 fruits and vegetables which contain the least amount of pesticides. These 15 produce items do not have to be purchased as organic. They are safe to consume as non-organic. Following these lists will not only help reduce inflammation brought on by toxins and pesticides, but it will save you money only having to purchase 12 types of organic produce as oppose to having to buy all organic produce.
- Consume cruciferous vegetables (veggies that are a part of the cabbage family)as a regular part of your weekly diet.
- If you drink any alcohol, opt for red wine as it also contains phytonutrients!
- For a treat, opt for dark chocolate (with a minimum cocoa content of 70%) as it contains phytonutrients from the cocoa plant.
- Whenever possible, opt for plant-based teas such as white or green tea as oppose to coffee as the tea contains phytonutrients.
- Whenever possible, include soy-based products: soybeans, soy milk, tofu, soy nuts, soy yogurt, etc. for heavy dose of phytonutrients

Vitamin & Minerals Intake on the Anti-Vitiligo/ Anti-Inflammatory Diet

Obviously, vitamins and minerals are needed in order to maintain optimum health. The ideal way to receive your recommended amount of vitamins and minerals is to eat a diet that is filled with fresh fruits and vegetables. Supplements are also an excellent way to ensure you are taking in the proper amount of vitamins and minerals daily. The following guidelines will help ensure you are getting enough vitamins and minerals in your diet.

- The easiest way to ensure you are getting the right amount of vitamins and minerals per day is to take a multivitamin/multimineral supplement each day with your largest meal. Look at the label and to make sure that the supplement contains at least:
  - → 400 micrograms of folic acid
  - → 2,000 IU of vitamin D
  - → No iron (unless you are a female with a regular menstrual cycle)
  - → No preformed vitamin A (retinol).
- Make sure you are getting at least 200 milligrams per day of vitamin C.

- Make sure you are getting at least 400IU of per day of vitamin E.
- Make sure you are getting at least 200 micrograms per day of an organic form of Selenium.
- Make sure you are getting at least 10,000-15,000IU per day of mixed carotenoids.
- Women should take 500-700 milligrams of supplemental calcium (preferably calcium citrate) per day. Men should avoid taking any supplemental calcium.

Water Intake on the Anti-Vitiligo/ Anti-Inflammatory Diet

Water consumption is so important and is a vital component to an anti-inflammatory diet. Pure, spring water acts as an anti-inflammatory just as well as taking 800mg of Ibuprofen, but there is no long-term risk to your liver when consuming water. Water coats and quells cellular inflammation, decreasing it until the cells return to normal size. Just as water puts out fire, it drives the inflammation out of the cells in our bodies.

Drinking enough water is essential for good health – our bodies are made up of nearly 70% water. Water helps our body function. It keeps us from becoming dehydrated. It helps carry oxygen throughout the blood and it helps in the disbursement/delivery of nutrients. It helps our bodies to maintain a safe internal body temperature, which keeps our organs healthy and thriving. When it comes down to it, nearly every biological function in our bodies in some way relies on proper water consumption. The following guidelines will help ensure you are consuming enough water in your diet.

- Women should attempt to consume at least 90-ounces of water per day.
- Men should attempt to consume at least 125-ounces of water per day.
- If you don't like drinking water or find that you have a hard time consuming your recommended daily amount of water, try sweetening your water with fresh fruit, lemons, or limes. Try meeting your daily water consumption through drinking lemonade, iced tea, flavored water, or sugar-free powders such as sugar-free or low-sugar Kool-Aid, Crystal Light, etc.
- 100% fruit juice is okay in moderation – it is best to dilute with water.
- If your tap water contains chlorine or other contaminants, opt for bottled water or a water-purifier as contaminants can irritate and trigger inflammation.

There you have it! These are the important components which make up an anti-inflammatory diet. You are now equipped with the knowledge needed to properly maintain an anti-inflammatory lifestyle.

As promised, the final part of this book contains recipes which will get you well on your way to becoming an anti-inflammatory expert. We have broken the recipes down in several convenient categories. Good luck and have fun experimenting with these deliciously simple recipes! Note: Many of the recipes can be manipulated to meet your family's taste preferences. Experiment with the recipes, substitute ingredients, but most of all have fun doing it! Just keep in mind that these recipes have been specially designed using a variety of ingredients that work together to help combat inflammation, so be cautious about how much you alter the recipes, but don't be afraid to gingerly make them to your own liking and, again, have fun!

PART TWO

The Recipes

Recipe Lingo

Throughout the recipes, you will see certain abbreviations and terms used repeatedly. If you are not cook on a regular basis, these terms and abbreviations may not make any sense. Below you will find a legend which lists the terms and abbreviations used frequently in the following recipes and what each means. If you have any trouble remembering, always refer to this legend.

Recipe Lingo Legend

Abbreviations/Measurements

tsp.	=	teaspoon
tbsp.	=	tablespoon
c.	=	cup
lb.	=	pound
oz.	=	ounce

Recipe Terms

Ingredient Cutting Terms

minced	=	smaller than 1/8-inch; cut into tiny pieces
diced	=	1/8-inch cubes
finely chopped/chopped fine	=	smaller than ¼-inch; cut into cubes
coarsely chopped	=	larger than ¼-inch; smaller than ½-inch; cut into cubes
Sliced	=	Cut thinly lengthwise; around ¼-inch in thickness
Cubes	=	To cut into cubes about ½-inch in size
Julienne	=	To cut into long, thin strips, matchstick-like in shape.

Note: The smaller the cut, the more quickly the item will cook; this can be the difference in a recipe of whether something is overcooked or still raw

Cooking Terms

Al Dente	=	Pasta cooked until just firm; typically 5 to 7 minutes after boiling.
Baste	=	To moisten food/meat to prevent food from drying out during cooking or to add flavor.
Beat	=	To stir rapidly and vigorously until mixture is smooth, using a spoon, whisk, or electric mixer.
Blanch	=	To cook briefly in boiling water then to seal in flavor and water (such as keeping asparagus bright green), to prepare for freezing or for easier skin removal.
Boil	=	To cook in hot, bubbling water that has reached a temperature of at least 212°F.
Blend	=	To combine two or more ingredients until smooth, either by hand with a spoon, electric mixer or immersion blender or by using a stand mixer/blender.
Broil	=	To cook on a rack in the oven, under or over direct heat.
Brown	=	To cook in a pan over medium-high to high heat, on the stove, until food is browned.

Caramelize	=	To heat sugar in a saucepan on the stove until it liquefies and turns into a syrup-form, ranging from golden in color to dark brown.
Core	=	To remove seeds/toughened center from fruits and vegetables (such as removing the core from an apple)
Cream	=	To beat together two or more ingredients, typically consisting of a sugar and a fat (such as granulated sugar and butter) until a creamy, smooth, and whipped mixture is formed.
Cut-in	=	To add a solid fat, such as butter, to flour or dry ingredients by adding it to the dry ingredients in small cut pieces or slices.
Dollop	=	A tablespoonful of a soft food, such as a dollop of yogurt or sour cream.
Dredge	=	To cover or coat uncooked food with flour, a cornmeal mixture or bread crumbs. Such as when preparing fried chicken.
Drizzle	=	To pour a liquid lightly back and forth over food in a fine stream. Such as drizzling vinaigrette over a salad.
Dust	=	To lightly coat with cocoa, powdered sugar, or another powdered ingredient.
Fillet	=	A flat piece of boneless meat, poultry, or fish. Also, to cut the bones from a piece of meat, poultry, or fish.
Fold	=	To combine light ingredients such as whipped cream or beaten egg whites with a heavier mixture, using a gentle over-and-under motion, usually with a rubber spatula.
Glaze	=	To coat foods in a glossy mixture such as a sauce or syrup.
Grate	=	To rub foods against a serrated surface to produce shredded or fine bits
Grease	=	To rub or spray the interior surface of a cooking dish or pan with cooking spray, olive oil, or other substance that will prevent food from sticking to the pan.
Grind	=	To reduce food to tiny particles using a grinder or a food processor.
Marinate	=	To soak in a flavored liquid; usually refers to meat, poultry, or fish.
Parboil	=	To partially cook by boiling. Usually done to prepare food for final cooking by another method.
Poach	=	To cook gently over very low heat in barely simmering liquid just to cover.
Purée	=	To mash or grind food until completely smooth, usually in a food processor, blender, sieve, or food mill.
Reduce	=	To reduce the amount of liquid by making it thicker and concentrating its flavor through boiling.
Roast	=	To cook a large piece of meat or poultry uncovered with dry heat in an oven.
Sauté or Panfry	=	To cook food in a small amount of fat over relatively high heat. Most of the recipes in this book use extra-virgin olive oil as the type of fat used.
Scald	=	To heat liquid almost to a boil until bubbles begin to form around the edge.
Sear	=	To brown the surface of meat by quick-cooking over high heat in order to seal in the meat's juices.
Shred	=	To cut food into narrow strips with a knife or a grater.
Simmer	=	To cook in liquid just below the boiling point; bubbles form but do not burst on the surface of the liquid.
Stew	=	To cook covered over low heat in a liquid.
Stir-Fry	=	To quickly cook small pieces of food over high heat, stirring constantly.
Whip	=	To beat food with a whisk or mixer to incorporate air and produce volume.
Whisk	=	To beat ingredients (such as heavy or whipping cream, eggs, salad dressings, or sauces) with a fork or whisk to mix, blend, or incorporate air.
Zest	=	The outer, colored part of the peel of citrus fruit. Such as the zest of a lime or lemon.

• • •

Note About Food Allergies and Substitutions

Each day more and more people are being diagnosed with food allergies. While many of the recipes in this holiday cookbook are gluten free, it is nearly impossible to predict what someone will be allergic to.

If you do have allergies I recommend that you research some of the possible substitutions to your allergens and alter the recipe to eliminate the reactive ingredients. Here are some excellent substitutions for several of the most common food allergies:

- ✓ Cow Milk
- ✓ Rice Milk
- ✓ Coconut Milk
- ✓ Hemp Milk
- ✓ Water
- ✓ Oat Milk
- ✓ Almond Milk

Note about Gluten Free Baking and Oils

Gluten = Glue

Since some of the recipes listed are gluten-free, there is less "glue" to hold the dough together. As a rule, gluten-free dough takes longer to combine. The best approach is to first make the dough and then to let it chill in the fridge for at least 60 minutes and up to 24 hours in order for it to properly set which will allow for more of a traditional dough-like consistency. Any recipes that may require this method throughout the E-book will be detailed in the recipe directions.

Oils

Fats are is an essential part of our diet. They are required for good health. I have done my best to offer healthy oil substitutions in this book, oil choices that are from butter, olive oil, grape seed oil, and coconut oil. I have selected these because of their higher cooking points and unrefined qualities. If you are not heating the oil, feel free to substitute avocado, walnut, or flax in place of the ones listed above.

Butter should always be purchased as organic due to the high concentration of Polychlorinated Biphenyls, (PCB's) that accumulate in butter fat.

~ *Breakfast Recipes* ~

Veggie Breakfast Wrap

Yield: 2 wraps
Servings: 2 (Serving Size: 1 wrap)
Total Time – Prep to Finish: 10 minutes

Ingredients

- 4 tbsp. red onion, chopped
- 4 tbsp. green bell pepper, chopped
- 4 eggs
- 1/8 c. fat free milk
- 2 (10-inch) whole-wheat flour tortillas

Directions

1. Place a small nonstick skillet over medium heat and spray lightly with cooking spray. Add in the bell pepper and onion and sauté for 1 to 2 minutes, or until both are tender and the onion translucent.

2. In a small bowl, crack in eggs and whisk. Add in milk; whisk until well-blended. Pour eggs into the pan and cook, stirring frequently until eggs are scrambled to your liking.

3. To serve, spoon half the egg mixture into each tortilla, wrap, and serve. Try serving with a side of fresh fruit for a complete meal.

Mini Omelet Soufflés with Mushrooms & Leeks

Yield: 4 soufflés
Servings: 2 (Serving Size: 1 soufflé)
Total Time – Prep to Finish: 30 minutes

Ingredients

- Extra-virgin olive oil cooking spray
- 1 stalk leeks - washed; sliced into 1-inch rounds
- 1 tbsp. extra-virgin olive oil
- 2 cloves garlic - minced
- 4-oz. gourmet mushroom blend (such as a mixture of shiitake, crimini, baby bella, oyster, etc.) - cut into small pieces with kitchen sheers
- Pinch of sea salt, to taste
- Pinch of white pepper, to taste
- ¾ c. frozen organic petite peas
- 2 tbsp. fresh basil – chopped fine
- 6 organic pastured eggs
- ¼ c. crumbled feta cheese (opt.)

Directions

1. Preheat oven to 375°F. Lightly spray 4 (1 cup) jumbo muffin cups or 4 (6 oz.) ramekins with olive oil spray.

2. In small-sized batches, place the leek rounds into a food processor and pulse to shred, then transfer shredded leeks to a separate bowl and set aside.

3. Place a large nonstick skillet over medium heat and add the olive oil and heat. When oil is hot, toss in the garlic and shredded leeks and sauté for 3 to 4 minutes, or until garlic is fragrant and leeks tender. Add in the mushrooms and sauté for an additional 2 minutes or until the mushrooms have begun to just barely wilt, then season with a pinch of sea salt and white pepper, more or less to taste. Next, add the peas to the pan and cook for 1 minute, then gently stir in the basil. Remove from heat.

4. Place the eggs, plus a second pinch each of sea salt and white pepper, more or less to taste, into a blender. Blend on high for 30 seconds.

5. Divide the leek-mushroom mixture into fourths, and place ¼ of the mixture into the center of each jumbo muffin cup or ramekin. Then carefully and dividing evenly, pour the egg mixture over the top of the leek-mushroom mixture in each jumbo mushroom cup or ramekin. Place in the preheated oven and bake for 15 minutes. Remove from oven and top each soufflé with 1 tbsp. each of crumbled feta (opt.). Return to oven and bake for 5 to 7 more minutes or until eggs are set and soufflés are lightly golden brown and puffy. Let cool for 5 minutes before serving.

• • •

Barley Breakfast Bowl with Lemon Yogurt Sauce

Yield: 2 breakfast bowls
Servings: 2 (Serving Size: 1 breakfast bowl with 2 tbsp. sauce)
Total Time – Prep to Finish: 10 minutes

Ingredients

- 1½ c. cooked barley, keep warm
- 1 c. mung bean sprouts (or preferred variety)
- 1/3 c. Cotija cheese or queso fresco - crumbled
- ¼ c. sliced almonds, toasted
- ¼ tsp. kosher salt
- 1 small avocado – peeled/pitted, and flesh diced or sliced
- ½ tsp. sea salt
- ¼ tsp. fresh ground black pepper

Lemon Yogurt Sauce

- 1 c. Greek plain yogurt
- 1 tsp. lemon zest, finely grated
- 1 tsp. fresh lemon juice
- ¼ c. fresh mint or parsley, chopped
- Sea salt, to taste
- Fresh ground black pepper, to taste

Directions

1. First, prepare the Lemon Yogurt Sauce: Combine the plain yogurt, lemon zest and juice, fresh mint or parsley, and salt & pepper in a bowl and stir to blend well. Cover and refrigerate until ready to serve.

2. Next, prepare the barley bowl: In a small mixing bowl, combine the barley, bean sprouts, cheese, almonds, and salt. Stir to mix well.

3. Divide barley mixture into 2 serving bowls. Top each barley bowl with 2 tbsp. lemon yogurt sauce and avocado. Add a pinch of salt and pepper, to taste, serve and enjoy!

Blackberry Griddle Pancakes
(Gluten-Free Recipe)

Yield: 12 pancakes
Servings: 6 (Serving Size: 2 griddle pancakes ¼ c. blackberry topping)
Total Time – Prep to Finish: 10 minutes

Ingredients

- 1 large egg
- 2 c. buttermilk
- ¼ c. pure maple syrup
- 1 c. gluten-free oat flour
- 2/3 c. yellow cornmeal
- 1/3 c. brown rice flour
- ¼ c. buckwheat flour
- 1 tbsp. baking powder
- 1 tsp. baking soda
- 1 tsp. kosher salt
- ¼ c. (½ stick) unsalted butter, melted
- 1 tbsp. extra-virgin olive oil

Blackberry Topping

- 4 c. fresh blackberries
- ½ c. honey

Directions

1. Prepare blackberry topping by placing a medium-sized saucepan over medium-high heat. Add in the blackberries and honey and stir to incorporate. Bring to a simmer and cook, stirring occasionally for about 10 minutes or until the blackberries begin to break down a bit and the mixture resembles a loose, syrupy jam. Add 1 tbsp. of water, if needed, to help the blackberry mixture become syrupy. If more water is needed, add more 1 tbsp. at a time. Remove from heat and set aside.

2. In a small-sized mixing bowl, whisk together the egg, buttermilk, and maple syrup. In a separate large-sized mixing bowl, combine the oat flour, buckwheat flour, cornmeal, brown rice flour, baking powder, baking soda, and salt and stir well to blend.

3. Stir the egg mixture into bowl with dry ingredients, then cut in butter and stir until smooth and there are no lumps.

4. Place a large nonstick skillet over medium heat and add in olive oil. When hot, pour ¼ c. of batter into the skillet. Cook 2 to 4 minutes or until bottom is browned and small bubbles begin forming on the top. Flip pancake over and cook for approx. 2 minutes or until browned and cooked through. Remove from skillet and repeat process until all of the batter has been used.

5. To serve, Place 2 pancakes onto each serving plate and top with 1/8 to ¼ c. blackberry topping. Serve and Enjoy!

• • •

Poached Eggs with Feta & Chickpeas in Tomato Sauce

Yield: 8 poached eggs and 4 – 6 c. tomato mixture
Servings: 6 (Serving Size: 2 poached egg and ½ to 1 c. tomato mixture)
Total Time – Prep to Finish: 35 minutes

Ingredients

- ¼ c. extra-virgin olive oil
- 1 medium white onion, chopped fine
- 4 garlic cloves, coarsely chopped
- 2 jalapeños – seeded, diced
- 1 (15-oz.) can chickpeas, drained
- 2 tsp. Hungarian sweet paprika
- 1 tsp. ground cumin
- 1 (28-oz.) can whole peeled tomatoes – crushed by hand, juices reserved
- ¼ tsp. kosher salt
- 1/8 tsp. fresh ground black pepper
- 1 c. feta cheese, crumbled
- 8 large eggs
- 1 tbsp. flat-leaf parsley, chopped
- 1 tbsp. fresh cilantro, chopped
- Warm pita wedges/bread, for dipping

Directions

1. Preheat oven to 425°F.
2. Place a large ovenproof skillet over medium-high heat. Add in olive oil and allow it to get hot, and then add in the onion, garlic, and jalapeños. Cook vegetables, stirring occasionally, for approx., 6 to 8 minutes or until the onion is tender and translucent and the garlic fragrant. Next, add in the chickpeas, paprika, and cumin. Cook for 2 more minutes, then add in the crushed tomatoes, along with the reserved juices, stir to combine. Bring contents to a boil and then reduce heat to medium-low and let simmer, stirring occasionally, for about 15 minutes or until sauce begins to slightly. Season with salt and pepper, to taste. Then, sprinkle crumbled feta evenly over the tomato sauce.
3. Next, carefully crack the eggs, one by one, into the tomato sauce mixture (taking care not to break the yolks); make sure the eggs are placed evenly apart.
4. Place skillet in preheated oven and bake for 5 to 8 minutes or until the whites of the eggs are set, but the yolks still runny. Remove from oven and place 2 eggs on each serving dish with ½ to 1 c. of the tomato mixture. Sprinkle on parsley and cilantro, to garnish, and serve alongside warm pita wedges or pita bread for dipping.

• • •

Porridge with Chia Seed-Blood Orange Yogurt Sauce

Yield: 2 cups
Servings: 2 (Serving Size: half of mixture)
Total Time – Prep to Finish: 10 minutes

Ingredients

- 4 tsp. chia seeds
- 2 c. blood orange juice
- 1 tbsp. agave syrup (or honey, if preferred)
- 2 blood oranges, peeled
- ½ c. Greek plain yogurt

Directions

1. To begin, place the chia seeds, agave syrup (or honey), and juice together in a bowl and stir to blend. Place in the refrigerator and let set for at least 30 minutes or until the chia seeds have entirely absorbed into the liquid mixture.

2. Segment the oranges with a sharp knife. Cut away the pith and membranes so that all that is left is the flesh.

3. To serve, divide the chia mixture between 2 serving bowls. Top each serving with ¼ c. yogurt and half of the blood orange segments. Serve immediately.

Cinnamon Breakfast Quinoa

Yield: 4 cups
Servings: 4 (Serving Size: 1 c. quinoa, 2 tbsp. each of walnuts & syrup)
Total Time – Prep to Finish: 35 minutes

Ingredients

- 1 c. quinoa (all red or mix of red, black, and white) washed & drained through mesh sieve
- 1½ c. water
- 2 cinnamon sticks
- ¼ tsp. kosher salt
- ¼ tsp. cinnamon, if needed to taste (opt.)
- 8 tbsp. pure maple syrup, to drizzle
- 8 tbsp. Walnuts, coarsely chopped, to garnish

Directions

1. In a medium-sized saucepan over medium heat, combine quinoa, water, cinnamon sticks, and salt. Stir to blend, cover with lid, and bring to a boil, stirring occasionally. Reduce heat to low and let simmer, covered and stirring occasionally, for about 20 minutes or until all water has absorbed. Remove pan from heat and let stand for 5 minutes.

2. Remove cinnamon sticks and fluff with fork, add cinnamon and salt now, if needed to taste. Divide among 4 bowls and garnish each serving with 2 tbsp. chopped walnuts. Then drizzle 2 tbsp. maple syrup over each serving. Serve hot.

Veggie & Feta Frittata

Yield: 1 frittata
Servings: 2 (Serving Size: ½ frittata; 2 wedges)
Total Time – Prep to Finish: 35 minutes

Ingredients

- 1 tsp. extra-virgin olive oil
- 8 cremini mushrooms, sliced thin
- ¼ c. shallots, sliced thin
- 4 spears asparagus, cut into 1-inch pieces
- 1 scallion, sliced thin
- ¼ c. peas
- 1 tbsp. fresh dill, chopped
- 4 egg whites, lightly beaten
- ½ c. reduced-fat feta cheese, crumbled
- Sea salt, to taste
- Fresh ground black pepper, to taste

Directions

1. Heat oven to 350°F.

2. Heat olive oil in a medium-sized ovenproof pan over medium-heat. Add in mushrooms and shallots and sauté for 5 to 7 minutes or until browned. Season with salt and pepper, to taste, then add in asparagus pieces, scalliuon, peas, and fresh dill. Stir to combine.

3. Crack egg whites into small bowl and whisk until lightly beaten. Pour beaten egg whites over the vegetable mixture in pan. Sprinkle the top of the mixture with crumbled feta. Place pan in preheated oven and bake for 15 to 20 minutes or until egg whites are set through.

4. Remove from oven and cut into fourths. Place 2 wedges on two serving dishes. Serve and enjoy!

Crispy Eggs with Piquillo Peppers

Yield: 4
Servings: 4 (Serving Size: 1 egg; ¼ of the pepper mixture)
Total Time – Prep to Finish: 25 minutes

Ingredients

- 1 tbsp. distilled white vinegar
- 4 extra-large eggs
- ¼ c. plus 2 tbsp. extra-virgin olive oil
- 4 garlic cloves, sliced thin
- 2oz. prosciutto, cut into strips 2-inches long and ¼-inch thick.
- ½ c. canned piquillo peppers (or jarred roasted red peppers), cut into ½-inch wide strips
- ½ c. dry sherry
- 2 tsp. fresh marjoram, chopped
- 1 tsp. kosher salt, plus more if needed for taste
- Fresh ground black pepper, to taste
- 1 c. panko breadcrumbs (or preferred breadcrumbs)
- ½ tsp. fresh thyme, chopped
- 2 large egg whites

Directions

1. To begin, line a baking sheet with plastic wrap.

2. Pour 2-inches of water into the bottom of a large skillet and place over medium-high to high heat. Bring water to a boil, then reduce heat to medium-low to hold simmer. Add in vinegar.

3. Break 1 of the extra-large eggs into a bowl or ramekin and immerse the bowl (or ramekin) in the pan of water to allow the egg to quickly slide out of the bowl and into the pan of water. Repeat process with remaining 3 eggs and cook the 4 eggs for about 3 minutes or until the whites are firm, but yolks runny. Using a slotted spoon, carefully move eggs to the plastic wrap-lined baking sheet. Trim off any tattered edges of the eggs with a knife and then slide eggs into a medium-sized bowl filled with ice water. Cover bowl and place in refrigerator to chill until cold.

4. Place a medium-sized skillet over medium heat and add in 2 tbsp. olive oil. Once oil is hot add in garlic and sauté for 1 minute or until fragrant. Add in prosciutto and sauté for 1 additional minute. Next, add in peppers, dry sherry, and marjoram and simmer for about 10 minutes or most of the liquid has evaporated. Season with salt and pepper and remove from heat.

5. Layout a kitchen towel onto a flat surface and transfer chilled eggs to towel using a slotted spoon.

6. In a medium-sized bowl, combine panko breadcrumbs, thyme, and 1 tsp. of salt. Stir to blend. Crack and place egg whites into a separate medium-sized mixing bowl and beat lightly with whisk. Gently roll a poached egg in the egg whites and then into the breadcrumb mixture (its fine if not all of the egg gets covered in the breadcrumb mixture). Place the coated egg on a plate and then repeat the process with remaining 3 eggs.

7. Add ¾ c. olive oil to a medium-sized skillet and place over medium heat. Once oil is hot, gently slide coated eggs into oil one by one. Cook for about 2 to 3 minutes or until coating turns to a golden brown in color, the transfer eggs with slotted spoon to paper towel-lined plate to drain. Sprinkle eggs with salt.

8. To serve, divide the pepper mixture among 4 serving dishes. Place 1 egg on top of the mixture on each plate and serve.

• • •

Greek Yogurt with Cherry-Almond Syrup Parfait

Yield: 2 parfaits
Servings: 2 (Serving Size: 1 parfait)
Total Time – Prep to Finish: 30 minutes

Ingredients

- 1 c. fresh black or red cherries, pitted
- 2 tbsp. almond syrup
- 2 tbsp. coconut palm sugar
- 1 tsp. fresh-squeezed lemon juice
- 2 c. Greek plain yogurt, stir to loosen
- 2 tbsp. sliced almonds, to garnish
- 4 tbsp. granola of choice, to garnish (opt.)

Directions

1. Place a saucepan over medium-high heat and combine cherries, almond syrup, sugar, lemon juice, and 1 tbsp. of water. Stir to combine and bring to a simmer, stirring constantly until sugar is dissolved. Continue simmering for about 5 more minutes or until liquid is starting to turn into a syrupy mixture, but the cherries are still holding form. Transfer mixture to a bowl and let cool for 5 minutes at room temperature, then place in refrigerator to chill until completely cold.

2. Place 1 cup of Greek yogurt into 2 serving bowls and spoon ½ of the cherries and their syrupy juices over the yogurt. Garnish with sliced almonds and/or granola, if desired. Serve immediately.

Easy Omega-3 Packed Granola

Yield: 6 cups granola
Servings: 24 (Serving Size: ¼ cup)
Total Time – Prep to Finish: 45 minutes

Ingredients

- 4 tbsp. walnut oil, divided
- ¾ c. packed dark brown sugar
- 2 egg whites, beaten
- ½ tsp. coarse kosher salt
- 3 c. old-fashioned oats (organic preferred)
- 1 c. walnut halves, chopped
- ½ c. flaxseed meal
- 1 c. dates, pitted and coarsely chopped
- ¼ c. honey

Directions

1. Preheat oven to 350°F. Brush a large, heavy baking sheet with 2 tbsp. walnut oil. In a large mixing bowl, combine the remaining 2 tbsp. of oil, brown sugar, egg white, and salt. Mix to blend well. Then add in oats, flaxseed, and walnuts and toss to coat well.

2. Spread mixture on to baking sheet. Place in oven and bake for 15 minutes, then stir granola mixture with spatula and bake 15 more minutes. Remove from oven again and sprinkle the chopped dates over the mixture and drizzle evenly with honey. Place back in oven and cook for 7 to 10 minutes longer or until granola is golden brown in color. Remove from oven and stir with spatula to loosen. Transfer to a clean baking sheet and let cool completely. Store in airtight container.

3. Try serving over yogurt, as cereal with milk or on its own as a delicious snack. Serving size is ¼ cup.

Strawberry Maple Breakfast Parfait

Yield: 6 parfaits
Servings: 6 (Serving Size: 1 parfait)
Total Time – Prep to Finish: 25 minutes

Ingredients

- 3½ c. strawberries, divided
- ¾ c. pure maple syrup, divided
- 6 c. Greek plain yogurt
- 1 tsp. fresh-squeezed lemon juice
- 12 tbsp. granola of choice

Directions

1. Place a 2 qt. saucepan over medium-high heat and combine 2 ¼ c. of the strawberries and ½ c. maple syrup and stir to mix well. Cook, stirring occasionally, for 3 to 8 minutes or until strawberries have burst. Transfer to an ice bath, stirring occasionally, until cooled.

2. Meanwhile, place Greek yogurt and ¼ c. maple syrup together in a bowl and beat with an electric mixer until well combined.

3. Remove strawberry mixture from ice bath and stir the lemon juice and remaining 1¼ c. strawberries into the chilled mixture.

4. Assemble the parfaits. Take 6 parfait glasses and begin by placing 2 tbsp. of the strawberry mixture into the bottom of each parfait glass. Add a1 tbsp. layer of granola over the mixture. Next, add 1 c. of the Greek yogurt mixture, followed by 2 tbsp. of strawberry mixture, and garnish with 1 tbsp. of granola.

Bran Pumpkin Muffins

Yield: One dozen muffins
Servings: 12 (Serving Size: 1 muffin)
Total Time – Prep to Finish: 10 minutes

Ingredients

- 1½ c. unprocessed oat bran
- ½ c. firmly packed brown raw cane sugar
- ½ c. all-purpose spelt flour, oat flour, almond flour
- 2 tsp. baking powder
- 1 tsp. pumpkin pie spice
- ¼ tsp. sea salt
- 1 c. cooked mashed pumpkin
- ½ c. skim almond, rice, hemp, oat milk
- 2 egg whites, lightly beaten
- 2 tbsp. coconut oil
- Cooking oil spray

Directions

- Preheat oven to 425° F.

- In a large bowl, combine bran, brown raw cane sugar, spelt flour, oat flour, almond flour, baking powder, pumpkin pie spice and salt. Blend well. Make a well in center of mixture. Set aside.

- In a second bowl, combine the mashed pumpkin, almond, rice, hemp, oat milk, beaten egg whites and coconut oil. Stir well. Add to dry ingredients, stirring just until moistened.

- Spray (2) 6 ct. muffin pans or (1) 12 ct. muffin pan with cooking oil spray or use paper liners. Spoon into the muffin tins until each is 3/4 full.

- Place in oven and bake for 14 to 16 minutes or until a toothpick poked into the center of a muffin comes out clean. Carefully remove the muffins from pans immediately; serve warm or at room temperature.

Cranberry & Orange Parfait

Yield: 2 parfaits
Servings: 2 (Serving Size: 1 parfait)
Total Time – Prep to Finish: 10 minutes

Ingredients

- 2 c. nonfat Greek yogurt
- 2 tsp. orange zest
- 1 tsp. vanilla extract
- 2 tsp. ground flaxseeds
- 2 orange, peeled and sliced (enough to make 2 cups)
- 2 Tbsp. dried cranberries
- 2 Tbsp. unsalted chopped walnuts

Directions

1. Combine yogurt, orange zest, vanilla and flaxseeds in a bowl. Blend Well. Spoon ½ c. of the yogurt mixture into two parfait dishes.

2. Layer each parfait dish with ½ c. orange slices, ½ tbsp. cranberries, and 1/2 tbsp. walnuts.

3. Next, top each dish with another 1/2 c. yogurt, followed by ½ c. orange slices, ½ tbsp.. cranberries, and ½ tbsp. walnuts. Serve immediately.

Asparagus & Gruyere Frittata

Yield: 1 frittata
Servings: 2 (Serving Size: 2 wedges)
Total Time – Prep to Finish: 12 minutes

Ingredients

- 1 tsp. extra-virgin olive oil
- ½ small onion, thinly sliced
- ½ pound asparagus, tough ends snapped off, spear cut diagonally into - 1-inch lengths
- 2 large eggs, lightly beaten
- Shredded Gruyere cheese, to garnish
- Salt and pepper, to taste

Directions

1. To begin, heat olive oil in a small (6 to 8-inch) oven-proof frying pan over medium-high heat.

2. When oil is hot, add onions to pan, add a pinch of salt to season. Cook onion, stirring occasionally, about 2 minutes or until onion begins to become tender and slightly translucent.

3. Add asparagus while reducing heat to medium-low. Cook, covered with lid, for about 5-6 minutes or until asparagus becomes slightly tender.

4. Next, pre-heat oven broiler. While broiler is heating, pour in eggs into pan and cook about 2 minutes until eggs are almost set, but still runny on the surface.

5. Sprinkle a little shredded Gruyere over to top of eggs to garnish. Place pan in oven and cook about 3-4 minutes or until cheese is melted and frittata is lightly browned. Remove from oven.

6. Slide Frittata onto serving plate and cut into half and then into fourths. Place 2 wedges on each plate and serve hot.

Egg Enchiladas

Yield: 2 enchiladas
Servings: 2 (Serving Size: 1 enchilada)
Total Time – Prep to Finish: 10 minutes

Ingredients

- 1 whole cage-free organic egg
- 3 cage-free organic egg whites
- 2 tbsp. organic Cheddar cheese
- 2 whole grain tortillas, sprouted grain tortillas, corn tortillas
- 1 organic avocado, sliced
- 1 c. organic salsa, divided

Directions

- Lightly coat skillet with cooking spray and place over medium heat.
- In a small bowl whisk together egg and egg whites until blended.
- Pour the eggs into the skillet and scramble for about 2 minutes.
- Add cheese and stir until eggs are set and cheese is melted.
- Lightly dampen two paper towels and place corn tortillas between them. Warm in oven.
- Fill each tortilla with 1/4 of the scrambled eggs, sliced avocado and a spoonful of salsa. Place 2 enchiladas per plate. Roll up and serve.

Berry Chocolate Protein Pancakes

Yield: 12 pancakes
Servings: 6 (Serving Size: 2 pancakes)
Total Time – Prep to Finish: 10 minutes

Ingredients

- 1 scoop chocolate protein powder
- 8 egg whites
- 3 c. rolled oats
- 3 tbsp. low fat cottage cheese
- 1 tbsp. agave nectar (or natural sweetener of choice)
- Enough water to reach a consistency of your liking
- 2 c. fresh mixed berries
- ½ tsp. cinnamon
- Cooking spray
- 6 tbsp. plain Greek yogurt

Instructions

1. Place the egg whites, rolled oats, cottage cheese, and agave nectar into a blender and process until smooth. Add the protein powder, process again. Now, add a little water at a time and process until the batter reaches a consistency of your liking.

2. Spray a large frying pan or griddle lightly with cooking spray and place over medium-low to medium heat. Pour ¼ c. batter onto griddle and let cook for about 2 to 3 minutes per side or until golden brown and cooked through. Repeat process with remaining batter to make the rest of the pancakes.

3. To serve, place two pancakes on each serving plate. Top pancakes with 1 tbsp. yogurt, 1/8 c. mixed berries, and sprinkle with cinnamon, to garnish. Serve and enjoy!

Strawberry-Oat-Chocolate Chip Muffins

Yield: 12 pancakes
Servings: 12 (Serving Size: 1 muffin)
Total Time – Prep to Finish: 30 minutes

Ingredients

- 1¼ c. whole wheat pastry flour
- 1 c. rolled oats
- ¾ tsp. baking soda
- ½ tsp. baking powder
- ¼ tsp. salt
- 1 heaping c. mashed bananas (about 2 to 3 large very ripe bananas)
- 1 tbsp. extra virgin olive oil
- 1 tbsp. honey or agave nectar
- 1 tsp. vanilla
- 1 egg
- 1 egg white
- 1/3 c. nonfat plain Greek yogurt
- ½ c. unsweetened vanilla almond milk
- 1/3 c. mini chocolate chips
- 2/3 c. diced strawberries
- 12 thin slices of strawberries (about 3-4 strawberries) for garnish, if desired

Instructions

1. Preheat oven to 350°F and lightly grease a standard 12-cup muffin pan or grease with paper liners. In a large-sized mixing bowl, combine flour, oats, baking powder, baking soda, and salt. Stir to blend. Reserve 2 tbsp. of mixture and set aside. In a separate large mixing bowl, combine mashed banana, olive oil, honey, and vanilla. Next, beat in the egg and egg white and beat until combined. Now add in Greek yogurt and almond milk and beat with an electric mixer on low until smooth.

2. Gradually add wet ingredients to dry ingredients and blend until just combined, but do not over mix the batter as it will make the muffins firm.

3. Fill each muffin cup 2/3 full of batter. Tap the pan gently on the counter to even out batter. Place a thin slice of strawberry onto each muffin, if desired. Place pan in preheated oven and cook for 18 to 23 minutes or until a toothpick inserted in the center of one of the muffins comes out clean. Remove from oven and let sit for 5 to 10 minutes in pan before placing on cooling rack to cool completely.

French Toast Casserole with Strawberries

Yield: 12 pancakes
Servings: 12 (Serving Size: 1 c.)
Total Time – Prep to Finish: 1 hour 15 minutes

Ingredients

- 6 c. cubed, whole grain bread
- 8 egg whites
- 1½ c. unsweetened almond milk
- ¼ c. honey (or maple syrup)
- 1 tsp. vanilla extract
- 2 tsp. almond extract
- 2 tsp. ground cinnamon
- 2 c. fresh strawberries

Instructions

1. Preheat oven to 350°F and grease a 9 x 13-inch glass casserole baking dish with oil. Place the bread cubes across the bottom of the baking dish.

2. In a large-sized mixing bowl, combine egg whites, honey, vanilla & almond extracts, and the cinnamon. Whisk until well combined. Pour the egg mixture over the bread and set aside for 30 minutes, stirring the mixture a couple of times to ensure that all the bread in coated in the egg mixture.

3. Fold in the strawberries.

4. Place the casserole in the preheated oven and bake 30 to 40 minutes or until set and cooked through, with no more liquid remaining. Let sit 5 minutes to cool before serving. Serving Size: 1 cup casserole.

Garden Fresh Breakfast Tarts

Yield: 6 tarts
Servings: 3 (Serving Size: 2 tarts)
Total Time – Prep to Finish: 25 minutes

Ingredients

- ¼ c. milk
- 1 large egg
- 3 large egg whites
- ½ tsp. fresh ground black pepper
- ½ tsp. sea salt
- ¼ c. broccoli, chopped
- ½ clove garlic, minced
- 2 medium mushrooms, chopped
- ½ small whole tomato, diced
- ¼ to ½ c. Italian-style bread crumbs
- ¼ c. mozzarella, finely shredded

Instructions

1. Begin by prepping 12-cup muffin pan. Use silicon trays, if you are able, as they will better prevent the eggs from sticking. If using regular pans, grease cups well with cooking spray. Preheat oven to 325 °F. Begin placing the crust by using a teaspoon and scooping a thin, even layer of breadcrumbs into the bottom of each muffin cup. Press the breadcrumbs down to create a muffin base that is ¼-inch thick.

2. Crack the eggs into a medium-sized bowl, add milk and beat well. Set aside. Prepare all of the vegetables and the mozzarella cheese by chopping, dicing, mincing, and shredding each according to the ingredient list. Combine the vegetables together in a separate bowl. Set cheese aside.

3. Pour half of the egg mixture into the bowl of vegetables and mix well. Divide the veggie mixture among each muffin cup by spooning a bit of the mixture over the top of the bread crumb base. Fill the muffin cups ¾ of the way full. Next, pour a little of the remaining egg mixture into each cup. If you need more, you may crack 1 more egg and 1/16 cup of milk and beat. However, do your best to spread the remaining egg mixture sparingly enough that you are able to fill each cup.

4. Finally, top each muffin cup with one teaspoon of finely-shredded mozzarella cheese. Let the tarts sit out for at least 10 minutes so that the egg mixture has time to seep into the breadcrumbs in order to seal the crust. Transfer muffin pan to the oven and bake at 325 °F for 5 to 7 minutes or until the tarts are golden brown on top and the cheese is melted. Place two tarts on a plate and sprinkle salt and pepper to taste. Enjoy hot.

Breakfast Pitas

Yield: 4 pitas
Servings: 4 (Serving Size: 1 pita)
Total Time – Prep to Finish: 15 minutes

Ingredients

- 8 egg whites
- 2 c. bell peppers, chopped (any color)
- 1 tsp. garlic powder
- 1 tsp. onion powder
- 1 c. raw spinach (but you can cook it if you prefer)
- 2 tsp. extra virgin olive oil
- 4 whole-wheat pita pockets

Instructions

1. Add the olive oil to a large sauté pan and place over medium heat. When the oil is hot in glistening, toss in the bell pepper and sauté for about 3 minutes or until tender. Add in the spinach now (if you want it cooked) and sauté for about 1 to 3 minutes or just until edges begin to wilt.

2. Place the egg whites into a small bowl, whisk well. Add in spices; whisk well. Pour the egg mixture into the sauté pan and scramble everything together.

3. Remove from heat and stuff ½ to 1 c. mixture into a pita pocket and serve.

Cool Melon Salad

Servings: 2
Total Time – Prep to Finish: 10 minutes

Ingredients:

- 1 large cantaloupe, peeled and seeded
- 3 tbsp. orange juice
- 3 tbsp. honey
- 1 c. red seedless grapes, halved
- 3 kiwi fruit, peeled, quartered and sliced
- 1/2 c. toasted coconut

Directions:

1) Cut 6 rings from the center of the cantaloupe. Place each ring on an individual salad plate and set aside.
2) Cut up the remaining cantaloupe and place in a large bowl with the rest of the ingredients.
3) Toss and spoon over the cantaloupe rings. Sprinkle with the coconut.

Pear Yogurt Smoothie

Servings: 2
Total Time – Prep to Finish: 3 minutes

Ingredients:

- 2 fresh pears, chopped
- 1 c. low-fat plain yogurt
- 1 banana, peeled
- 3 ice cubes, crushed
- 2 tbsp. honey
- Dash ground nutmeg
- 1 scoop of protein powder

Directions:

1. Combine pears, yogurt, banana, ice and honey in blender or food processor; blend until smooth.
2. Add protein powder and blend until no sign of the powder remains.
3. Pour into two glasses. Sprinkle with nutmeg and serve immediately to receive full nutritional value.

Strawberry Scones

Yield: 10 scones
Servings: 10 (Serving Size: 1 scone)
Total Time – Prep to Finish: 25 minutes

Ingredients:

- Cooking oil spray
- 1/4 c. raw cane sugar
- 2 c. all-purpose spelt flour, oat flour, or almond flour
- 1 tbsp. baking powder
- 1/4 tsp. salt
- 1/4 tsp. baking soda
- 1 tbsp. grated orange zest
- 1/4 c. non saturated fat butter
- 1/2 c. almond butter
- 1/4 c. cage free eggs or egg whites
- 1 tsp. vanilla
- 1 c. frozen strawberries

For the Glaze

- 3/4 c. powdered raw cane sugar
- 1/4 tsp. grated orange zest
- skim almond, rice, hemp, oat milk

Directions:

1. Preheat oven to 400°F. Spray a nonstick cookie sheet with cooking oil spray.
2. In a large mixing bowl, combine raw cane sugar, choice of flour, baking powder, salt, baking soda and orange zest.
3. Cut in butter with a pastry cutter or fork until mixtures forms coarse crumbs.
4. Stir together cage free eggs and vanilla. Add to crumb mixture and stir until just moistened.
5. Stir in the strawberries and blend well.
6. Gently transfer dough to cutting board coated lightly with spelt flour, oat flour, or almond flour. Knead approximately 14 times or until dough is smooth.
7. Form into a 7-inch circle on the cookie sheet and cut into 10 wedges.
8. Place in preheated oven and bake for 14 to 15 minutes or until scones become slightly golden. Remove from oven and let cool for 5 minutes.
9. While scones cool, prepare the glaze. In a small bowl mix together the powdered raw cane sugar, orange zest, and just enough milk (of choice) to form a glaze of drizzling consistency.
10. Drizzle the glaze over top of scones and serve warm. Serving size equals one scone.

Vanilla Nut Cereal

Servings: 2
Total Time – Prep to Finish: 10 minutes

Ingredients:

- 3 tbsp. Cream of Wheat cereal
- 1 scoop vanilla protein powder
- 1/8 to 1/4 c. water
- 1/4 tsp. of cinnamon
- natural cane sugar, to taste

Directions:

1. In a medium-sized pan, prepare Cream of Wheat cereal as directed on Package.

2. Once the Cream of Wheat is ready, stir in the scoop of vanilla protein powder and the cinnamon. If the protein powder makes the Cream of Wheat too thick, stir in some of the water - a little at a time until the desired consistency is reached. Transfer the cereal to two separate bowls and sprinkle on natural cane sugar, to taste, if preferred. Serve immediately.

Oatmeal Scramble:

Servings: 2
Total Time – Prep to Finish: 10 minutes

Ingredients:

- 4 scrambled cage-free organic eggs
- 1 c. of rolled oats
- 1/4 tsp. ground cinnamon
- 1/4 tsp. ground nutmeg
- 2 c. water
- 1 organic apple, unpeeled and coarsely shredded
- 2 tsp. maple syrup or raw honey

Directions:

1. Place a non-stick skillet over medium to medium-high heat. In a small mixing bowl, crack and whisk together the organic eggs. Pour the eggs into the skillet and cook, stirring frequently, until scrambled.

2. In a medium-sized saucepan over medium-high heat, combine the water and the shredded apple pieces. Bring the contents to a boil.

3. In a separate small bowl, combine the oats and the spices. Blend thoroughly. Stir the oats mixture into the boiling water. Reduce heat to medium-low and cook 5 minutes stirring frequently.

4. Divide the scrambled eggs and transfer among two breakfast plates. Divide the oatmeal and place that alongside the eggs on each plate. Drizzle the eggs and oatmeal lightly with maple syrup or raw honey, if desired. Serve immediately.

Greek Yogurt, Berries, & Honey Parfait

Yield: 2 parfaits
Servings: 2 (Serving Size: 1 parfait)
Total Time – Prep to Finish: 5 minutes

Ingredients

- 2 c. plain Greek yogurt (or flavor of choice)
- 4 tsp. honey
- 1/2 c. fresh sliced strawberries, plus 4 extra slices as garnish (opt,)
- 1/2 c. fresh strawberries

Directions

1. Mix the berries together in a small bowl.

2. Using two parfait dishes, place 1/3 c. of Greek yogurt in the bottom of each dish. Next place 1/4 c. of the berries mixture into each parfait dish. Drizzle 1 tsp. of honey into each dish, followed by another 1/3 c. yogurt, followed by a second 1/4 c. of the berries followed by the final 1/3 c. of yogurt into each dish.

3. Garnish each parfait with 2 slices of strawberry and 1 tsp. of honey. Serve Immediately

Strawberry-Bran Breakfast Sundae

Yield: 2 wraps
Servings: 2 (Serving Size: 1 wrap)
Total Time – Prep to Finish: 10 minutes

Ingredients

- 2 c. vanilla or lemon-flavored low-fat yogurt (preferably Greek yogurt) or flavor of choice.
- 2 c. bran flakes
- 1/4 c. fresh strawberries
- 2 tbsp. sliced almonds (or nuts of choice)
- 2 tbsp. chopped pecans (or nuts of choice)
- 2 tbsp. dried cranberries (or dried or fresh fruit of choice)

Directions

1. In a bowl, place 1 c. yogurt and one c. bran flakes.

2. Top with 1/8 c. fresh strawberries, followed by 1 tbsp. each of slice almonds, chopped pecans, and dried cranberries.

3. Repeat with remaining ingredients to make second serving. Serve immediately.

Eggs with Kale & Apple

Servings: 2 (Serving Size: half)
Total Time – Prep to Finish: 10 minutes

Ingredients

- 4 c. kale, chopped
- 1 clove garlic, chopped
- 2 to 3 tbsp. coconut oil
- Juice from half a lemon
- 4 eggs
- 1 Granny Smith apple (or apple of choice), cored and cut into wedges
- Sea salt and fresh ground black pepper, to taste

Directions

1. Begin by chopping the kale very finely. Chop the clove of garlic.
2. Melt 1 to 2 tbsp. of coconut oil in a large pan over medium heat. Add the garlic and sauté for 2 minutes, stirring frequently.
3. Add the chopped kale and cook for 4 more minutes, stirring frequently.
4. Squeeze the lemon juice onto the kale and blend together. Push the kale to one side of the pan so that it stays out of the way but remains hot.
5. Heat the remaining coconut oil in the empty half of the pan. Crack the eggs into the pan and fry for 1 to 2 minutes per side, until desired doneness is reached.
6. Divide the kale among two plates. Place two eggs on top of the kale on each plate. Arrange the apple wedges alongside the eggs. Sprinkle with sea salt and pepper to taste and serve.

Scrambled Eggs & Veggie Bowl

Yield: 2 bowls
Servings: 2 (Serving Size: 1 bowl)
Total Time – Prep to Finish: 15 minutes

Ingredients

- 4 eggs, scrambled.
- 1/2 c. red peppers, sliced
- 1/2 c. thinly sliced zucchini
- 1/8 c. white onion, chopped
- 1/4 c. mushrooms, sliced
- 2 to 4-ounces cheddar cheese, shredded (or cheese of choice)

Directions

1. In a skillet, scramble the four eggs. When the eggs are barely set, add in all the vegetables and 2-ounces shredded cheese. Cook until veggies are tender, eggs are completely set, and cheese is melted, approximately. 3 to 4 minutes.

2. Divide the eggs between two plates and sprinkle a little of the remaining cheese over each dish. Serve immediately.

Cinnamon-Apple Granola with Greek Yogurt

Servings: 2
Total Time – Prep to Finish: 15 minutes

Ingredients

- 1/2 c. raw almonds, chopped (or raw nuts of choice)
- 1/2 c. raw walnuts, chopped (or raw nuts of choice)
- 1/2 apple, peeled and diced
- 1 tbsp. almond flour
- 2 tbsp. vanilla protein powder
- 1 tsp. ground cinnamon
- 1/8 c. applesauce, unsweetened preferred
- 2 tsp. honey
- 2 tsp. almond butter
- 1/16 tsp. vanilla extract
- dash of sea salt
- 1 cup Greek plain or vanilla yogurt (or flavor of choice)

Directions

1. In a mixing bowl, combine the chopped almonds, chopped walnuts (or preferred raw nuts), diced apple, vanilla protein powder, almond flour, lucuma (opt.), cinnamon, and salt in a bowl. Mix well.

2. In a second bowl, combine the apple sauce, almond butter, honey, and vanilla extract. Mix well. Pour the bowl with the nuts into the bowl with the wet ingredients and blend together thoroughly. Make sure all dry ingredients get coated.

3. Place the granola mixture onto a parchment paper-lined baking sheet and bake until desired crunch is obtained. Approximately 8 to 10 minutes. Remove from oven and let cool or eat hot. Place 1/2 c. each of Greek yogurt into two bowls. Divide the granola and sprinkle over the yogurt in each bowl. Serve immediately.

Huevos Rancheros

Yield: 2 wraps
Servings: 2 (Serving Size: 1 wrap)
Total Time – Prep to Finish: 10 minutes

Ingredients

- (2) 8-inch whole wheat tortillas
- 2 hard-boiled eggs, sliced
- 2 slices of Canadian bacon or ham
- 1-ounce slice of cheddar cheese
- 2 tbsp. salsa

Directions

1. Prepare the hardboiled eggs.
2. Place one tortilla on a plate, top with a slice of Canadian bacon or ham, the sliced egg, and a slice of cheddar cheese. Roll the tortilla up. Repeat with remaining ingredients to prepare second burrito.
3. Serve immediately with 1 tbsp. salsa

Oatmeal-Applesauce Muffins

Yield: 1 dozen muffins
Servings: 12 (Serving Size: 1 muffin)
Total Time – Prep to Finish: 40 minutes

Ingredients

Topping
- 1/4 cup rolled oats
- 1 tbsp. brown sugar
- 1/8 tsp. cinnamon
- 1 tbsp. unsalted butter, melted

Muffins
- 1 c. old fashioned rolled oats (not instant)
- 1 c. nonfat milk
- 1 c. whole wheat flour
- ½ c. brown sugar
- ½ c. unsweetened applesauce
- 2 egg whites
- 1 tsp. baking powder
- ½ tsp. baking soda
- ½ tsp. salt
- ½ tsp. cinnamon
- ½ tsp. sugar
- raisins or nuts (opt.)

Directions

1. To begin, first presoak the oats in milk for 1 hour,

2. Preheat oven to 400°F and grease a standard 12-cup muffin pan with cooking spray or use paper liners.

3. In a mixing bowl, combine oat-milk mixture, applesauce, and egg whites. Blend well and set aside.

4. In a separate bowl, combine whole wheat flour, brown sugar, baking powder, baking soda, salt, sugar, and cinnamon.

5. Gradually add wet ingredients to dry ingredient and blend until just combined, but do not over mix the batter as it will make the muffins firm. Add raisins or nuts (opt.).

6. Prepare topping: In a small bowl, whisk together the oats, brown sugar, and cinnamon. Add in melted butter and toss gently with fork to coat ingredients.

7. Fill each muffin cup 2/3 full of batter. Sprinkle topping on the top of each batter-filled muffin cup. Tap the pan gently on the counter to even out batter. Place muffin pan in preheated oven and cook for 20 to 25 minutes or until a toothpick inserted in the center of one of the muffins comes out clean. Remove from oven and let sit for 5 minutes before serving.

Banana-Oatmeal Vegan Pancakes

Yield: 12 pancakes
Servings: 4 (Serving Size: 3 pancakes)
Total Time – Prep to Finish: 20 minutes

Ingredients

- 1¼ c. old fashioned oats
- ½ c. organic whole wheat flour
- 2 tsp. baking powder
- ½ tsp. sea salt
- 1½ c. soymilk*
- 2 ripe bananas

Directions

1. To begin, heat griddle or skillet over medium heat.

2. Next, place all ingredients, except for banana, into a blender and process until smooth. Add the bananas to blender and blend until smooth.

3. Lightly grease griddle with olive or coconut oil then pour ¼ c. of batter onto griddle and cook for 2 to 3 minutes, then flip and cook for about 2 minutes or until the pancake is golden brown and cooked through.

4. Repeat process with remaining batter.

5. Place 3 pancakes on each serving dish, serve alongside preferred toppings, and enjoy. Yield: 1 dozen medium-sized pancakes.

Peanut Butter-Banana Muffins

Yield: 1 dozen muffins
Servings: 12 (Serving Size: 1 muffin)
Total Time – Prep to Finish: 40 minutes

Ingredients

- 1½ c. all-purpose flour
- 1 c. old-fashioned oats
- 1 tsp. baking powder
- ½ tsp. baking soda
- ½ tsp. salt
- 2 tbsp. applesauce
- ¾ c. light brown sugar
- 2 large eggs
- 1 c. mashed banana (about 3 bananas)
- 6 tbsp. creamy peanut butter
- 1 c. low-fat buttermilk

Directions

1. Place a small nonstick skillet over medium heat and spray lightly with cooking spray. Add in the bell pepper and onion and sauté for 1 to 2 minutes, or until both are tender and the onion translucent.

2. In a small bowl, crack in eggs and whisk. Add in milk; whisk until well-blended. Pour eggs into the pan and cook, stirring frequently until eggs are scrambled to your liking.

3. To serve, spoon half the egg mixture into each tortilla, wrap, and serve. Try serving with a side of fresh fruit for a complete meal.

~ *Lunch Recipes* ~

Pita Pizza with Eggplant

Yield: 2 pizzas
Servings: 2 (Serving Size: 1 pizza)
Total Time – Prep to Finish: 10 minutes

Ingredients

- 2 whole-wheat pita pockets
- 1/2 c. marinara sauce, low sodium
- 1 c. shredded mozzarella
- 1/2 c. eggplant, diced
- 1/2 c. tomato, diced
- 1/2 c. onion, sliced
- 1/4 c. button mushrooms, sliced

Directions

- Spread a thin layer of marinara sauce on a pita pocket. Top the sauce with 1/2 c. shredded mozzarella, followed by the 1/4 c. eggplant, 1/4 c. tomato, 1/4 c. onion, and 1/8 c. mushrooms. Repeat with second pita pocket and remaining ingredients to make second pizza. Bake pizzas in a preheated oven or toaster oven for 5 to 7 minutes or until cheese is melted and edged are becoming browned.

- Place each pizza on a plate and serve immediately.

Taco Salad

Yield: 4 salads
Servings: 4 (Serving Size: 1 salad)
Total Time – Prep to Finish: 15 minutes

Ingredients

- 2-lb extra-lean ground beef (4 c. cooked)
- ½ head of lettuce, shredded – enough to make 6 cups
- ½ mango, peeled, seeded, and cut into chunks
- ½ tomato, chopped
- ½ avocado, peeled, seeded, and sliced
- ½ red onion, sliced
- 2 c. baked tortilla chips, crumbled
- 6 tbsp. lime juice
- 4 tbsp. extra-virgin olive oil

Directions

1. Brown ground beef in a medium-sized pan over medium heat. Drain. Set aside.

2. On a plate, arrange 1½ c. shredded lettuce. Top with 1 c. of ground beef, 1/4 of each of the following toppings: mango, tomato, avocado, and onion.

3. Sprinkle ½ c. crumbled baked tortilla chips over the salad. Drizzle 1 ½ tbsp. lime juice and 1 tbsp. olive oil over the salad.

4. Repeat process with remaining ingredients to make the remaining salad. Serve immediately.

Baby Spinach Salad with Smoked Salmon

Yield: 2 salads
Servings: 2 (Serving Size: 1 salad with 4oz. salmon)
Total Time – Prep to Finish: 15 minutes

Ingredients

- 1 c. romaine washed and separated.
- 4 c. fresh baby spinach leaves, washed.
- 6 cherry tomatoes
- 2 hard-boiled eggs, sliced
- 2 slices red onion, chopped
- 1 tbsp. capers (opt.)
- 8 oz. smoked salmon, split.
- 2 tbsp. red wine vinaigrette dressing (or alternative organic salad dressing of choice)

Directions

1. In a salad bowl, arrange 1/2 c. romaine and 2 c. baby spinach. Place 4 oz. smoked salmon on top of salad greens. Garnish salad with 3 cherry tomatoes, 1 sliced egg, 1 slice chopped red onion, and 1/2 tbsp. capers (opt.).

2. Repeat with remaining ingredients to build second salad.

3. Drizzle 1 tbsp. red wine vinaigrette dressing (or preferred organic dressing) over each salad and enjoy. Leftovers can be stored in fridge, covered, for up to 48 hours.

Grilled Chicken and Baby Arugula Salad with Apple, Walnuts, and Goat Cheese

Yield: 2 salads
Servings: 2 (Serving Size: 1 salad and 4 oz. grilled chicken)
Total Time – Prep to Finish: 15 minutes

Ingredients

- 2 tbsp. extra-virgin olive oil
- 1 medium shallot, peeled and sliced
- ½-lb. (8oz.) fully cooked grilled chicken breast strips, cut into cubes OR left as strips – whichever preferred
- ½ tart green apple, thinly sliced
- 2 c. baby arugula leaves
- ¼ c. toasted walnuts, coarsely chopped, to garnish
- 2 tbsp. crumbled goat cheese, to garnish
- 1 tsp. Lemon Juice, for salad dressing
- 2 tbsp. extra-virgin olive oil, for salad dressing
- Salt and Pepper, to taste

Directions

1. Drizzle 1 tbsp. olive oil in a non-stick skillet over medium heat. When the oil becomes hot and shimmery, but not to the point of smoking, add the sliced shallot to the skillet. Sauté in the oil 1-2 minutes or until it become translucent. Remove from skillet and set aside. Place another 1 tbsp. of olive oil in the skillet and add the grilled chicken. Heat the chicken for about 4 minutes, stirring on occasion, until the chicken is heated through. Remove chicken from pan and chill.

2. Take a medium-size mixing bowl and combine sliced shallot, chicken pieces, sliced apple, and baby arugula. Toss together to blend well.

3. Divide and transfer among two salad dishes. Drizzle 1 tbsp. of olive oil and 1/2 tsp. of lemon juice over each salad. Add a pinch of salt and pepper, to taste.

4. Finally, garnish each salad with 1 tbsp. crumbled goat cheese and 1/8 c. toasted chopped walnuts. Serve immediately.

Avocado & Shrimp Salad

Yield: 2 salads
Servings: 2 (Serving Size: 1 salad and 6 oz. shrimp)
Total Time – Prep to Finish: 15 minutes

Ingredients

- 1-lb. (12 oz.) small to extra-small shrimp – cooked, peeled, and de-veined
- 1/8 c. white wine vinegar
- 1/8 c. extra-virgin olive oil
- ½ to 1 green onion, sliced extra thin
- 1 to 2 ripe avocado, peeled and cut into chunks
- 4 large lettuce leaves, (preferably butter or red leaf lettuce)
- 1/4 c. Roasted walnuts or pistachios, to garnish
- 1/2 tbsp. chopped cilantro, to garnish
- 4 lemon wedges, to garnish

Directions

1. In a small bowl, blend oil, vinegar, and sliced green onion.

2. Slice shrimp into ½-inch pieces and add oil mixture and toss to coat shrimp with oil mixture.

3. Arrange lettuce leaves on individual serving dishes.

4. Prepare avocado by cutting the avocado in half and removing the pit. Remove some of the avocado around the pit area and mix in with the shrimp.

5. Using a spoon, scoop out the avocado halves from its skin in one piece.

6. Place an avocado half on each plate with lettuce.

7. To finish, scoop the shrimp mixture onto the avocado on each plate. Sprinkle with roasted walnuts and cilantro; add a wedge of lemon or two, to garnish (if desired). Serve immediately.

Chicken & Asparagus Sandwich

Yield: 2 sandwiches
Servings: 2 (Serving Size: 1 sandwich)
Total Time – Prep to Finish: 10 minutes

Ingredients

- 1-lb. fresh asparagus, trimmed and cut into 3-inch pieces
- 1 1/2 c. fat free sour cream
- 2 tsp. lemon juice
- 1 1/2 tsp. prepared mustard
- 1/2 tsp. salt
- 8 oz. sliced cooked chicken breast
- 4 sprouted grain, spelt, rice bread English muffins, split and toasted
- 2 medium tomatoes, sliced
- Paprika, to taste

Directions

- Place asparagus in a saucepan and cover with water; bring to a boil. Cover and cook for 2 minutes or until crisp-tender. Drain and set aside.

- In the same pan, combine the sour cream, lemon juice, mustard and salt; cook on low until heated through. Remove from the heat.

- Place chicken on a microwave-safe plate; microwave on high for 45-60 seconds or until warmed.

- Place two English muffin halves on each serving plate. Top with chicken, tomatoes, asparagus and sauce. Sprinkle with paprika, if desired. Serve immediately.

Radicchio Orange and Arugula Salad

Yield: 2 salad
Servings: 2 (Serving Size: 1 salad)
Total Time – Prep to Finish: 10 minutes

Ingredients

- 2 medium-size seedless oranges
- 2 tbsp. orange juice
- 2 tbsp. olive oil
- 1 tbsp. white wine vinegar
- 2 tsp. walnut oil
- 1/2 tsp. grated orange peel
- 1 medium-size head Radicchio, torn in bite size pieces
- 1 large bunch arugula, ends trimmed
- 1/4 c. walnuts, toasted, chopped

Directions

1. Using sharp knife, cut away all peel and white pith from oranges. Cut oranges crosswise into 1/4-inch thick slices. Cut each slice in half. Set aside.

2. Whisk juice, olive oil, vinegar, walnut oil and orange peel in medium bowl to blend. Season with salt and pepper.

3. Combine endive, arugula and orange slices in large bowl. Add vinaigrette and toss to coat.

4. Divide among two salad bowls and sprinkle each bowl with 1/8 c. chopped walnuts.

White Bean Salad

Yield: 2 salads
Servings: 2 (Serving Size: 1 salad)
Total Time – Prep to Finish: 15 minutes

Ingredients

- 1 c. dry white pea beans, soaked and cooked according to directions
- 2 large stalks celery, sliced diagonally
- 1 small onion, chopped
- 1 small green or red pepper, sliced
- 1/2 c. sliced ripe olives (optional)
- 1 c. cherry tomatoes, halved (optional)
- 3 tbsp. coconut oil
- 5 tbsp. vinegar
- 1/4 c. raw cane sugar
- 1/2 tsp. dry mustard
- 1/4 tsp. garlic powder
- 1/2 tsp. salt
- Pinch paprika

Directions

1. Combine cooked beans, celery, onion, green or red pepper, olives and tomatoes (opt) in a large bowl. Set aside.
2. In a second bowl, mix remaining ingredients together and pour over bean mixture; mix well. Cover and refrigerate until ready to eat.

Fresh Fruit & Yogurt Salad

Yield: 2 salads
Servings: 2 (Serving Size: 1 salad)
Total Time – Prep to Finish: 10 minutes

Ingredients

- 1/2 c. plain low fat yogurt
- 1/4 c. fresh lime juice
- 1/4 c. honey
- 1 tsp. grated fresh lime peel
- 2 c. diced peeled cantaloupe
- 2 c. diced peeled honeydew melon
- 1 c. seedless red or green grapes
- 1 c. fresh strawberries
- 2 c. diced peeled cored fresh pineapple
- 1 c. raspberries or blackberries
- 1 1/2 c. halved hulled strawberries

Directions

1. First, prepare the dressing. In a bowl, whisk together the yogurt, lime juice and honey. Blend well and set aside.

2. Wash and prepare the fruits. Place the fruit in a bowl and pour the yogurt dressing over the fruit. Toss and stir to cost. Let stand for a few minutes at room temperature to allow the flavors to blend.

3. Divide between two dishes and serve. Best when served chilled.

Rice-Stuffed Tomatoes

Yield: 2 stuffed tomatoes
Servings: 2 (Serving Size: 1 stuffed tomato)
Total Time – Prep to Finish: 35 minutes

Ingredients

- 6 large fresh tomatoes at room temperature
- 2 tbsp. olive oil
- 1 1/2 c. sliced fresh white mushrooms
- 1 c. chopped onion
- (1) 10-ounce package frozen chopped spinach, thawed and drained
- 2 tsp. minced garlic
- 1 tsp. dried basil leaves, crushed
- 1/2 tsp. salt
- 1/4 tsp. ground black pepper
- 1/2 c. brown rice
- 1/4 c. plus 2 tablespoons grated Parmesan cheese

Directions

- Preheat oven to 400°F. Use tomatoes that are fully ripe. Cut a slice from the top of each tomato; remove pulp, leaving a 1/4-inch thick shell; set aside.

- Chop up the tomato pulp (makes about 3-1/2 cups). Set aside.

- In a large skillet over high heat. Heat the olive oil until hot. Add mushrooms and onion; cook and stir until tender, about 3 to 4 minutes.

- Add spinach, reserved chopped tomatoes, garlic, basil, salt and pepper. Cook over low heat, stirring occasionally, until flavors blend, about 10 minutes. Stir in rice. Remove from heat; cover and let stand for 5 minutes. Stir in 1/4 cup Parmesan cheese. Place tomato shells in a 13 × 9 × 2-inch baking pan. Spoon hot mixture into shells, dividing evenly. Sprinkle 1 teaspoon Parmesan cheese on top of each. Bake until tomatoes are hot and filling is golden, about 15 minutes. Divide between two dishes and serve hot.

Aloha Chicken Kabobs

Yield: 12 kabobs
Servings: 4 (Serving Size: 3 kabobs)
Total Time – Prep to Finish: 20 minutes

Ingredients

- 3/8 c. reduced sodium soy sauce
- 3/8 c. brown raw cane sugar
- ¼ c. sherry
- 2 tbsp. sesame oil
- ½ tsp. ground ginger
- ½ tsp. garlic powder
- ½ tsp. organic honey or honey of choice
- 6 skinless, boneless chicken breast halves - cut into 2-inch pieces
- (2) 20-ounce cans pineapple chunks in juice, drained
- 12 Skewers (soak wooden skewers in water before using)
- High-heat cooking spray

Instructions

1. In a shallow glass dish, mix the soy sauce, brown raw cane sugar , sherry, sesame oil, ginger, and garlic powder.

2. Stir the chicken pieces and pineapple into the marinade until well coated.

3. Preheat grill to medium-high heat.

4. Lightly oil the grill grate. Thread chicken and pineapple alternately onto skewers.

5. Grill 5 to 7 minutes, turning occasionally, or until juices run clear. Place 3 skewers onto each serving plate and enjoy!

Shrimp Tacos with Greek Yogurt Sauce

Yield: 6 tacos
Servings: 3 (Serving Size: 2 tacos)
Total Time – Prep to Finish: 25 minutes

Ingredients

- Olive oil cooking spray
- 2 tbsp. salsa
- 4 whole-wheat tortillas
- 1 1/2 limes juiced
- 1 lime, peel intact – cut into wedges
- 6-ounces small shrimp – tail on, fully cooked
- 1/2 c. plain Greek yogurt
- 1/4 tbsp. plus 1 tsp. dried cumin
- 1/4 tsp. ground oregano
- 1/2 tbsp. cayenne pepper
- 1/4-ounce dill
- 2 c. cabbage, shredded
- 1/2 c. fresh cilantro, torn or chopped
- 1 clove garlic, minced
- 1/8 c. any preferred low-calorie mayonnaise

Instructions

1. In a skillet, coated with olive oil cooking spray, sauté shrimp for 2 minutes over medium to medium-high heat. Add in fresh minced garlic, 1 tsp. dried cumin, 1 tbsp. salsa, and the juice from 1 lime.

2. Prepare the yogurt sauce: In a medium-sized mixing bowl combine yogurt, mayo, oregano, remaining cumin, dill, and cayenne pepper.

3. Prepare cilantro, lime, and cabbage as directed. Warm tortillas in the microwave or oven. Fill warm tortillas with sautéed shrimp, shredded cabbage, fresh cilantro, ¼ of the yogurt sauce and serve alongside 2 tbsp. salsa and a couple lime wedges. Serving size is 2 tacos.

Spinach Portobello Pizza Caps

Yield: 8 pizza caps
Servings: 4 (Serving Size: 2 caps)
Total Time – Prep to Finish: 20 minutes

Ingredients

- 8 Portobello mushroom caps; washed well, dried, and stems removed
- 2/3 c. tomato sauce
- 1 c. baby spinach leaves, torn
- 1 1/3 tbsp. fresh garlic, minced
- 1/3 c. black olives, sliced
- 1/3 c. green bell pepper, sliced (or can be cut into chunks or diced)
- 1/3 c. red onion, chopped
- A few cherry tomatoes, sliced (use preferred amount for each pizza)
- 1 c. mozzarella cheese, finely shredded (will use 2 tbsp. per pizza)
- 30 spinach leaves
- Fresh or dried basil, to garnish (opt.)
- 1/2 tbsp. dried Italian seasonings

Instructions

1. Preheat oven to 375°F. Line a baking sheet with parchment paper. Prepare the mushroom caps as directed and place each mushroom, cap side up, on the baking sheet and place in oven to bake for 5 minutes. While the mushrooms are baking, place the tomato sauce in a small, shallow bowl. Add dried Italian seasonings and blend well. Prepare other ingredients as directed.

2. Remove mushroom caps from oven and spoon or brush the tomato sauce over the center of each cap. Next, layer each cap with 2 tbsp. of finely shredded mozzarella, followed by a few baby spinach leaves, cherry tomatoes, olives, green bell pepper, chopped red onion, and garlic.

3. Place caps in oven and bake 12 to 15 minutes or until cheese is melted and edges are golden. Garnish each pizza cap with fresh or dried basil (opt.) and transfer two caps to a serving dish. Enjoy while hot! Place raw baby spinach in a small bowl. Sprinkle the spinach with garlic and balsamic dressing. Toss to coat. Arrange baby spinach leaves on a salad dish. Top with grilled or boiled shrimp. Enjoy!

Toasted Strawberry and Goat Cheese Sandwich

Yield: 1
Servings: 1 (Serving Size: 1 sandwich)
Total Time – Prep to Finish: 10 minutes

Ingredients

- 2 slices whole wheat bread
- 1-oz. goat cheese, softened
- 1/4 c. sliced fresh strawberries
- 1 tsp. balsamic vinegar
- 1/4 c. fresh baby spinach or arugula
- Aluminum foil

Instructions

1. To begin, spread the softened goat cheese over one slice of bread.

2. Then top cheese with strawberries; drizzle vinegar over strawberries. Top with spinach and remaining slice of bread.

3. Place sandwich in toaster oven and cook for 1 to 3 minutes or until bread is toasted and a light golden brown. Serve hot.

Turkey Taco Wraps

Yield: 2 stuffed tomatoes
Servings: 2 (Serving Size: 1 stuffed tomato)
Total Time – Prep to Finish: 35 minutes

Ingredients

- 1-pound lean ground turkey or beef
- 1 c. 1 (4 oz.) can green chiles
- 1/2 tbsp. taco seasoning
- 1 (15 oz.) can corn, drained
- 1 (15 oz.) can black beans, rinsed and drained
- head lettuce or 6 low carb tortillas
- *Optional toppings:* low fat plain Greek yogurt or low fat sour cream, additional salsa for serving, corn, black beans, sliced olives

Instructions

1. Spray a large skillet with cooking spray and place over medium-high heat. Add in ground turkey, salsa, green chiles, and taco seasoning. Stir to combine. Cook for 8 to 12 minutes or until turkey is completely browned. Remove from heat and add corn and beans, stir to combine.

2. Prepare lettuce wraps: Cut off base of head of lettuce and cut in half lengthwise. Peel off individual leaves and wash and then pat dry using a paper towel. Scoop ½ c. of meat mixture into lettuce wraps and then top each wrap with Greek yogurt or sour cream, salsa, and olives, if desired.

3. Next, layer on the turkey, cheese, bacon, tomato, and lettuce (or spinach). Finally, fold in each side of wrap or tortilla and then roll up and enjoy!

Asian Snap Pea Salad

Servings: 2
Total Time – Prep to Finish: 20 minutes

Ingredients:

- 1 tbsp. oyster sauce
- Salt to taste
- 1 pound raw cane sugar snap peas, trimmed
- 1/2 c. carrots, cut into matchstick strips
- 1/2 c. drained sliced water chestnuts
- 1/2 c. sliced mushrooms, slightly sautéed beforehand
- 1/2 c. julienne cut red bell peppers
- 2 tsp. sesame seeds, toasted

Directions

1. To prepare dressing, heat oil in a small sauce pan over med heat, add ginger; sauté 2 minutes.
2. Add garlic and red pepper, cook 1 minute more.
3. Stir in oyster sauce, soy sauce, raw cane sugar and salt bring to a simmer.
4. Remove from heat, cool.
5. Sautee the mushrooms in a little broth, wine or water just until cooked.
6. To prepare the salad, steam or cook peas in boiling water 30 seconds. Drain and rinse in cold water.
7. Combine blanched peas and remaining ingredients except sesame seeds.
8. Drizzle dressing over salad, toss well. Transfer to 2 salad plates. Sprinkle with toasted sesame seeds. Serve.

Turkey Couscous Salad:

Ingredients:

- 3/4 c. water
- 1/2 c. couscous
- 1/4 tsp. ground cumin
- 3/4 tbsp. minced fresh parsley leaves
- 1 3/4 c. fully cooked boneless turkey breast, cut into 3/4-inch cubes
- 1 1/4 c. red seedless grapes, halved
- 2 tbsp. fresh pink grapefruit juice
- 1/2 tbsp. fresh lemon juice
- 1/4 c. packed fresh basil leaves (washed, patted dry, and chopped fine)
- 1 3/4 c. arugula (washed, patted dry, and stems removed)
- 2 tbsp. walnuts, toasted and chopped

Directions:

1. Place a small saucepan over medium-high to high heat and bring the water to a boil. Once a good boil is reached, reduce heat and stir in the couscous. Cover the saucepan with lid and let the couscous stand for 5 minutes.
2. Next, stir in the cumin, parsley, and salt (to taste) with a fork. Let the couscous mixture cool at room temperature for 5 more minutes.
3. In a separate bowl, toss together the turkey, grapes, juices, basil, as well as the salt and pepper, to taste.
4. To serve, arrange arugula on 2 separate dinner plates and divide couscous among them. Top the couscous with turkey mixture and any liquid remaining in the bowl over salads. Garnish each dish with 1 tbsp. toasted walnuts. Serve immediately.

Avocado Nicoise Salad

Yield: 2 salads
Servings: 2 (Serving Size: 1 salad)
Total Time – Prep to Finish: 10 minutes

Ingredients

- 1 can tuna (choose a tuna canned in water)
- 3/4 c. medium to large black olives, pitted
- 3/4 green onion, finely chopped
- 2 hard-boiled eggs, peeled and cut into wedges
- 3 sundried tomatoes, shredded
- 1/2 ripe avocado, cut into chunks
- 1/2 tbsp. lemon juice
- 1/2 tbsp. extra-virgin olive oil
- 1/2 tbsp. red wine vinegar
- 1/2 clove garlic, minced
- pinch of sea salt, to taste
- pinch of fresh ground black pepper, to taste

Directions

1. In a medium-sized bowl, combine the onion, tomato, avocado, and olives. Mix well.

2. In a second small bowl, prepare the salad dressing by whisking together the olive oil, vinegar, lemon juice, and minced garlic.

3. Drizzle the salad dressing over the avocado mixture and stir to thoroughly blend.

4. Next, add the tuna and stir to blend. Divide the salad among two separate salad plates. Arrange one egg's worth of wedges onto each plate. If desired, sprinkle on a pinch of sea salt and black pepper, to taste. Serve immediately.

Turkey Bacon Melt Sandwich

Yield: 2 sandwiches
Servings: 2 (Serving Size: 1 sandwich)
Total Time – Prep to Finish: 10 minutes

Ingredients

- 6 strips organic/natural turkey bacon, cut in half
- 2 sprouted whole-grain English muffin
- 4 thick slices of organic tomato
- 4 slices of organic cheese

Directions

1. Preheat oven to 400°F.

2. Prepare turkey bacon according to package directions.

3. Split the English Muffins in half and place the muffin halves face-up on a baking sheet.

4. Layer only two of the halves with 3 half-slices of bacon, followed by a slice of cheese, followed by 3 half-slices of bacon, followed by the remaining second slice of cheese. Place the baking sheet in the preheated oven and bake for 3-5 minutes or until the muffins are toasted and the cheese melted.

5. Remove the baking sheet from the oven and place 1 to 2 thick slices or tomato on the top of two of the muffin halves. If desired, place the baking sheet back in the oven and continue baking for an additional 3-4 minutes or until the tomato slices are warm.

6. Remove from oven and transfer the layered half of the English muffins onto two separate breakfast plates. Top each layered-half of muffin with the remaining non-layered halves to complete the sandwich. Serve immediately.

Poached Chicken Salad

Yield: 2 salads
Servings: 2 (Serving Size: 1 salad)
Total Time – Prep to Finish: 20 minutes

Ingredients

- 2 boneless, skinless chicken breasts, diced
- 1 tomato, cut into chunks
- 1 mango, cut into chunks
- 1 red capsicum, chopped
- 1 avocado, cut into chunks
- 1 beetroot, peeled and thinly sliced
- 6 asparagus spears
- 1/2 c. of roasted cashews
- 2 c. baby spinach
- 2 tbsp. + 1/4 c. extra-virgin olive oil
- 1 tbsp. + 1 1/4 tbsp. balsamic vinegar
- 1 organic, gluten free stock cube
- 2-3 c.s. water
- 1 tsp. white vinegar
- 1 tsp. dijon mustard

Directions:

1. Place the stock cube into a pot of water (using 2-3 c.s water or the amount of water directed on the stock cube package) and bring to a boil. Once a roaring boil is reached, add the chopped chicken to the pot and poach the chicken over high heat for approximately 5 minutes or until cooked through.
2. Remove the chicken from the heat and drain the water immediately. Transfer the chicken to a bowl and set aside.
3. Place 1 tbsp. olive oil and 2 tsp. balsamic vinegar in a non-stick pan and place the pan over medium heat. Place the asparagus spears and boot root into the pan and cook for approximately 5 minutes or until heated through and tender.
4. Prepare the salad dressing: In a small mixing bowl, whisk together the 1/4 c. olive oil, 1 1/4 tbsp. balsamic vinegar, 1 tsp white vinegar, and 1 tsp. dijon mustard until thoroughly blended. Set aside.
5. In a separate mixing bowl, combine the tomato chunks, mango chunks, avocado chunks, chopped capsicum, as well as the cooked asparagus and beetroot. Gently, stir and toss to blend contents thoroughly.
6. Assemble the salad: On the center of a serving plate, place 1 c. baby spinach. Divide the diced poach chicken and place half over the baby spinach. Place half of the tossed salad contents over the baby spinach and diced poached chicken. Drizzle half over the salad dressing over the entire salad and sprinkle on 1/8 c. of roasted cashews to garnish. Repeat process with remaining ingredients to prepare the second salad. Serve immediately.

● ● ●

Tuna-Stuffed Tomatoes

Yield: 2 stuffed tomatoes
Servings: 2 (Serving Size: 1 stuffed tomatoes)
Total Time – Prep to Finish: 10 minutes

Ingredients

- 1 medium tomato
- 1 6oz. can tuna, drained and flaked
- 2 tbsp. mayonnaise
- 1 tbsp. celery, chopped
- ½ tsp. Dijon mustard
- ¼ tsp. seasoning salt
- Shredded mild cheddar cheese, to garnish

Directions

1. Preheat oven to 375°. Wash tomato and cut in half from stem. Using a tsp., scoop out tomato pulp and any seeds until you have two ½" shells remaining.

2. In small mixing bowl, combine tuna, mayonnaise, celery, mustard, and seasoning salt. Stir until well blended.

3. Scoop an equal amount of tuna mixture into each ½ tomato shell. Place on baking sheet and sprinkle shredded cheddar cheese over the top each tuna-stuffed tomato shell. Bake for 7 to 8 minutes or until cheese is melted and golden-brown in color.

4. Serve immediately. Any remaining mixture can be safely stored, covered, in the fridge for up to 72 hours.

Greek Feta Lamb Burgers with Cucumber Sauce

Yield: 2 wraps
Servings: 2 (Serving Size: 1 wrap)
Total Time – Prep to Finish: 10 minutes

Ingredients
2 large garlic cloves, roasted, unpeeled, (bottled minced garlic optional)
¼ c. crumbled feta cheese
2/3 lb. (10oz.) ground lamb
¼ tsp. dried oregano
¼ tsp. sea salt
¼ tsp. ground black pepper

Cucumber Sauce

½ medium cucumber – peeled/grated, excess juice squeezed completely into bowl.
3 oz. sour cream (plain yogurt optional)
¼ tsp. fresh mint leaves, minced (dried mint optional)
½ tsp. red or rice wine vinegar
1 tbsp. minced garlic
2 tomato slices, thinly sliced
2 red onion slices, thinly sliced
2 c. mixed salad greens or fresh spinach.

Directions

1. In small nonstick skillet over medium heat, place 2 whole garlic clove, cook for about 4 – 5 minutes or until cloves form brown spots. Remove from skillet, cool to handle then peel, mince, and set aside.

2. In a mixing bowl, break up ground lamb. Add roasted garlic, feta cheese, oregano, salt, and pepper to meat. Stir until well blended then divide into 2 portions. Make 2 meat patties about 4-inches wide, Set aside in refrigerator.

3. In a small mixing bowl, prepare cucumber sauce, by combining cucumber, sour cream (or yogurt), mint, vinegar, and minced garlic. Add salt and pepper to taste. Mix until well blended. Set aside in refrigerator.

4. Remove lamb patties from fridge and grill over medium-high heat, about 4 to 5 minutes per side, turning only once, to reach medium-well/medium burgers.

5. To serve, arrange 1 c. salad greens or spinach on plate, next place onion slice, tomato slice, and feta-lamb burger. Top dish with 1 tbsp. cucumber sauce.

Crab & Pear Salad

Yield: 2
Servings: 2
Total Time – Prep to Finish: 10 minutes

Ingredients

- ¾ to 1 c. fresh lump crabmeat
- 1/8 c. toasted hazelnuts, chopped
- 1/4 c. celery, chopped fine
- 1 firm and sweet pear, chopped fine
- 1/8 c. red onion, chopped fine
- 1 tbsp. fresh parsley, chopped fine
- 1 tbsp. lemon juice
- 1 tbsp. extra-virgin olive oil
- Freshly ground pepper, to taste
- Sea salt, to taste
- 2 large leaves of butter lettuce, rinse and patted dry

Directions

1) In a medium-size salad bowl, combine the toasted hazelnuts, chopped celery, pear, onion, parsley, as well as lemon juice and olive oil. Sprinkle in sea salt and black pepper to lightly season. Blend well.

2) Next, gently fold in lump crabmeat, being careful not to break down the larger pieces of crabmeat.

3) To serve, arrange a large butter lettuce leave on a plate, then scoop crab salad on to the bed of lettuce. Sprinkle with additional sea salt and pepper, if needed for taste. Serve cold.

Banana-Nut Butter Sandwich

Yield: 2 sandwiches
Servings: 2 (Serving Size: 1 sandwich)
Total Time – Prep to Finish: 5 minutes

Ingredients

- 4 slices of whole-wheat bread
- 4 tbsp. nut butter
- 2 banana, sliced
- 2 tbsp. Agave nectar

Directions

1. Toast the slices of bread and place on a plate

2. Spread 1 tbsp. of nut butter onto each slice.

3. Arrange 1 sliced banana onto the toast.

4. Drizzle 1 tbsp. agave nectar over the banana and sandwich the two slices of toast together. Repeat with remaining ingredients to make second sandwich. Serve immediately.

Chicken Caesar Salad

Yield: 2 salads
Servings: 2 (Serving Size: 1 salad; 4 oz. grilled chicken)
Total Time – Prep to Finish: 10 minutes

Ingredients

- 8-ounces fully cooked grilled chicken breasts strips
- ½ tsp. extra-virgin olive oil
- Pinch sea salt, to taste
- Pinch freshly ground black pepper, to taste
- 4 c. romaine lettuce, washed and torn
- 1 medium to large red bell pepper, cut into strips to make 1 c.
- 1/4 c. Caesar salad dressing, divided
- Grated parmesan cheese, to garnish
- ½ lemon, cut into wedges

Directions

1. Combine the romaine and red bell pepper in larger mixing bowl and toss with Caesar dressing to coat.

2. Divide among two salad plates and top salad with 4oz of grilled chicken strips and grated parmesan. Serve immediately with lemon wedges.

Chicken Salad Stuffed Tomatoes

Yield: 2 stuffed tomatoes
Servings: 2 (Serving Size: 1 stuffed tomatoes)
Total Time – Prep to Finish: 5 - 10 minutes

Ingredients

- 1½ c. (6oz.) cooked boneless, skinless chicken breast, chopped into ¼-inch cubes
- 2 chilled medium tomatoes - tops cut off, pulp and seeds scooped out to form an empty shell.
- 1/8 c. toasted walnuts, coarsely chopped
- 1/2 stalk celery, finely chopped
- 1/2 tsp. lemon juice
- 1/4 c. mayonnaise
- 1/2 to 1 tsp. dried tarragon OR 1/2 to 1 tbsp. fresh chopped tarragon
- Salt and pepper, to taste

Directions

1. In a medium-sized mixing bowl combine the chicken cubes. Toasted walnuts, chopped celery, a splash of lemon juice, mayonnaise, and tarragon. Mix until well blended.
2. Add salt and pepper to season. Carefully spoon chicken salad mixture into the tomato shells and serve immediately.

Cashew-Garlic Grilled Chicken Wraps

Yield: 2 wraps
Servings: 2 (Serving Size: 1 wrap)
Total Time – Prep to Finish: 10 minutes

Ingredients

- 2 whole-wheat tortillas
- ½ c. roasted (salted or unsalted) cashews
- 3 tbsp. roughly chopped cilantro (leaves and stems)
- 1/8 c. extra-virgin olive oil
- 2 garlic cloves, roughly chopped
- 1 tbsp. soy sauce
- 1 tsp. brown sugar
- ½ jalapeno pepper, stems and most seeds discarded
- ½ tbsp. lime juice, plus lime wedges for garnish
- Kosher salt and ground pepper
- (4) bone-in, skin-on chicken thighs (½-1lb.)

Directions

1. In a food processor, combine the garlic, cilantro, soy sauce, brown sugar, jalapeno, lime juice, and 2 tbsp. of water. Pulse for about 30 seconds or until the ingredients form a smooth paste. Add salt and pepper to taste. Reserve a 1/3 of the paste to serve with the chicken. Use the remaining paste to coat the chicken thighs with the marinade.

2. Add a sprinkle of salt and pepper over the chicken thighs and then place the chicken thighs in a bowl and pour the paste over the chicken, making sure that the chicken thighs are very well coated with the marinade.

3. Preheat broiler or prepare grill for direct heat on medium to medium-high. Place room temperature marinated chicken in broiler or on grill and cook, turning frequently, until chicken is golden crisp and reaches an internal temperature of 170°F when inserted into the thickest part of the thigh.

4. To serve, transfer 2 thighs to serving dish alongside reserved marinade and garnish with cilantro and a lime wedge, if desired. Serve immediately

All-American Cobb Salad

Yield: 2 salads
Servings: 2 (Serving Size: 1 salad)
Total Time – Prep to Finish: 10 minutes

Ingredients

- 2 c. Romaine lettuce, Chopped
- 2 c. Boston Lettuce, chopped
- 1/2 small bunch of frisée (curly endive)
- 1/4 bunch of watercress, coarse stems discarded
- 4 slices of bacon
- 1 ripe avocado, seeds removed, peeled, and cut into ½-pieces,
- 1½ c. boneless, skinless cooked chicken, cut into ½-inch cubes
- 1/2 tomato, seeds removed and finely chopped
- 2 hard-boiled egg, separated, yolks and whites finely chopped. Keep separated
- 1 tbsp. fresh chives
- 4 tbsp. red wine vinegar
- 2 tsp. Dijon mustard
- Salt and pepper, to taste
- 1/3 c. olive oil
- Finely grated Roquefort, to garnish

Directions

1. Begin by prepping all the greens, make sure that it is all rinsed, spun (or patted) dry, and coarsely chopped. Place the bacon in a skillet and cook over medium heat until the bacon is crisp on both sides. About 3 to 5 minutes. Remove bacon from heat, let cool, then crumble. Set aside.

2. Place all of the various lettuces and watercress in to a large salad bowl then toss together. Divide the greens among two salad plates.

3. Divide the salad toppings and arrange the salad toppings over the two salads. Top each salad with ¾ c. chicken and half of the bacon crumbles.. Lay out the tomato and the avocado. Then garnish the salad with the diced eggs and chives.

4. Prepare the salad dressing. In a shallow bowl, whisk together the vinegar, mustard, and salt and pepper, to taste. Slowly add the oil, stirring until the mixture becomes emulsified. Stir in the Roquefort. Whisk the dressing until all is well blended.

5. To serve, transfer Cobb salad to a serving dish and serve salad dressing on the side or toss in with the salad. Serve chilled.

● ● ●

Avocado Crab Salad with Mango Sauce

Yield: 2 salads
Servings: 2 (Serving Size: 1 salad)
Total Time – Prep to Finish: 10 minutes

Ingredients

For the sauce:

- 1/2 tbsp. extra-virgin olive oil
- 1/4 ripe mango – peeled, pitted, and diced
- 1/8 c. water
- 1/2 tsp. freshly squeezed lemon juice
- Sea Salt and freshly ground pepper, to taste

For the salad:

- 1/2 lb. fresh lump Dungeness crabmeat, picked through to remove any shell fragments.
- 3/4 tbsp. freshly squeezed lime juice
- 2 tbsp. extra-virgin olive oil
- 1/2 tbsp.. cilantro leaves, finely chopped
- 1 tsp. mint leaves, finely chopped
- 1/2 tbsp. minced shallot or purple onion
- 1/2 medium size mango – peeled, pitted, and diced
- 1 firm, but ripe avocado – peeled, pitted, and diced
- 1/2 ruby red grapefruit – peeled and sectioned.
- 10 drops Tabasco sauce, to taste
- Sea salt and pepper, to taste

Directions

1. Prepare the sauce. Heat the olive oil in a small-size pan over medium heat. Add the mango and season with a sprinkle of salt and pepper. Cook for approximately 3 minutes or until the mango is tender. Pour in the water and bring contents to a boil, then immediately remove from heat. Stir in lemon juice. Transfer mango mixture to a blender and purée until creamy and smooth. Place in refrigerator to chill until time for use.

2. In a medium-size bowl, combine the crabmeat, half of the cilantro, half tsp. of the mint, shallot, 1/2 tbsp. of the lime juice, 1 tbsp. olive oil, 5 drops tabasco sauce, sea salt and pepper, to taste. Blend gently with a fork, and avoid breaking up larger pieces of crabmeat. Set aside.

3. In a separate small bowl, combine the avocado and mango, 1 tbsp. olive oil, 1/4 tbsp. lime juice, the remaining mint and cilantro, 5 drops tabasco sauce, sea salt, and pepper to taste. Carefully blend together, being cautious not to mush the avocado.

4. To serve, spoon 1/2 c. avocado mixture onto a chilled plate. Arrange 3oz. crabmeat on top of the avocado mixture, Garnish with cilantro leaves and place sectioned ruby red grapefruit around the crab salad. Serve ¼ c. mango sauce on the side. Serve immediately,

Grilled Salmon Salad

Yield: 2 salads
Servings: 2 (Serving Size: 1 salad)
Total Time – Prep to Finish: 45 minutes

Ingredients

- 1/2 lb. (8oz.) cooked grilled salmon, cooled to room temperature. (May also use poached or fried salmon as a substitute for grilled)
- 1 celery stalk, chopped fine
- 1/4 red onion, peeled and sliced very thin
- 1/2 tbsp capers, (strain out pickling juice)
- The juice of 1/2 a lemon
- 1/2 tbsp. extra-virgin olive oil
- 1 tbsp. fresh dill, chopped
- Sea salt and fresh ground pepper, to season
- 2 large Bibb lettuce leaves

Directions

1) In a salad bowl, break up grilled salmon into bite-size chunks. In a separate small bowl, combine celery, red onion, capers, lemon juice, olive oil, and fresh dill and blend very well. Softly add the dressing mixture to the bowl of salmon pieces and toss gently until all of the salmon is coated in the dressing mixture. Sprinkle with sea salt and pepper to season.

2) Place in refrigerator for about 30 minutes to allow the salad to chill and the flavors to blend well.

3) To serve, transfer to serving dish and garnish with 1 or 2 lemon wedges.

Steak & Arugula Salad

Yield: 2 salads
Servings: 2 (Serving Size: 1 salad)
Total Time – Prep to Finish: 10 minutes

Ingredients

For the Salad:

- Olive oil, canola oil, or grape seed oil, for cooking
- 1/2 lb. (8oz total) flank (or skirt) steak
- Salt and fresh ground pepper, to season
- 3 c. lettuce greens
- 1 c. baby arugula, tough stems removed
- 1/4 of a red bell pepper, sliced thin and cut into 1-inch pieces
- 2 scallions, sliced thin
- 2 tbsp. chopped walnuts, to garnish
- 2-ounces crumbled goat cheese, to garnish
- 1 tsp. pomegranate seeds, to garnish

For the Dressing:

- 2 tsp. lemon juice
- 2 tbsp. extra-virgin olive oil
- Salt and pepper, to taste

Directions

1. Using a cast-iron pan over high heat, heat 2 tsp. of olive oil in pan. Prepare the steak for grilling by patting dry with a paper towel and sprinkling each side with salt and pepper to season. Place the steak in the pan and sear for just a few minutes on each side until the steak is nicely browned on both sides, or until desired doneness is reached. Transfer steak to a cutting board and let rest for a few minutes before proceeding. Next, cut steak into thin slices, cutting against the grain of the flank steak.

2. In a medium-size salad bowl, toss together lettuce greens, arugula, bell pepper, and scallions. Spread out 1 c. of salad greens on each individual serving dish. Arrange 4oz. of steak slices on top of salad greens. Sprinkle with chopped walnuts, crumbled goat cheese, and pomegranate seeds, to garnish.

3. In a small, shallow bowl mix together olive oil and lemon juice, as well as a dash of salt and pepper. Mix well and then drizzle a little onto each salad. Serve immediately.

• • •

Sweet Potato Rounds with Rosemary-Butter Sauce

Yield: 2 wraps
Servings: 2 (Serving Size: 1½ c.)
Total Time – Prep to Finish: 20 minutes

Ingredients

- 1 large (2 small) sweet potatoes, washed and sliced into 1/2-inch rounds
- 2 tbsp. butter, melted
- 1 tsp. fresh rosemary, chop fine
- 1/4 tsp. garlic powder
- sea salt, to taste

Directions

1. Preheat grill to low.

2. Wash sweet potatoes and cut into ½-inch rounds; place rounds on a piece of aluminum foil.

3. In a small bowl, melt butter and stir in finely chopped rosemary and garlic powder until contents are well-blended.

4. Using a spoon, drizzle the rosemary-butter sauce mixture over each sweet potato round, both sides.

5. Add sea salt to the tops of sweet potato rounds and transfer rounds to the preheated grill. Grill the rounds on low for about 5 minutes each side.

6. Remove from grill and serve hot.

CranCherry Chicken Wraps

Yield: 2 wraps
Servings: 2 (Serving Size: 1 wrap)
Total Time – Prep to Finish: 10 minutes

Ingredients

- 2 multigrain or whole-wheat flat bread or tortillas
- 6-ounces fully-cooked, seasoned chicken breast strips, chopped fine
- 2 tbsp. sundried tomatoes, chopped
- 1 tbsp. dried cherries
- 1 tbsp. dried cranberries
- 2 tbsp. plain nonfat Greek yogurt
- 1 c. shredded lettuce
- pinch of kosher salt and black pepper to taste
- 2 tsp. tarragon vinegar

Directions

1. In a small-sized mixing bowl, combine chopped chicken breast, sundried tomatoes, dried cherries and cranberries, Greek yogurt, shredded lettuce, a pinch each of salt and pepper (more or less, to taste), and 1 to 2 tsp. of tarragon vinegar. Stir ingredients together until well-blended.

2. Scoop half of the mixture onto a piece of flat bread or tortilla, roll and place on serving dish. Repeat process with remaining mixture and another piece or flat bread or tortilla. Serve immediately.

Turkey Club Wraps

Yield: 1 wrap
Servings: 1 (Serving Size: 1 wrap)
Total Time – Prep to Finish: 10 minutes

Ingredients

- 1 flatbread wrap or whole wheat tortilla
- 2-ounce of smoked turkey (sliced deli-thin)
- ½ slice sharp American cheese (sliced deli-thin)
- 2 slices cooked bacon
- 1 tbsp. ranch yogurt dressing
- 2 tomato slices
- romaine lettuce (or baby spinach)

Directions

1. Begin by spreading ranch dressing out over the center of the wrap or tortilla.

2. Next, layer on the turkey, cheese, bacon, tomato, and lettuce (or spinach).

3. Finally, fold in each side of wrap or tortilla and then roll up and enjoy!

~ *Dinner Recipes* ~

Ginger Chicken with Mango Chutney and Toasted Almonds

Yield: 2
Servings: 2 (Serving Size: 1 chicken breast; half of mango chutney mixture)
Total Time – Prep to Finish: 15 minutes

Ingredients

- 2 boneless, skinless chicken breast halves
- 1 tsp. ground coriander
- ½ tsp. fresh ginger, grated
- 1/8 c. fresh ginger, julienned
- 4 tsp. grapeseed oil or other high flash point oil such as canola oil
- 1 tsp. white-wine vinegar
- ¼ tsp. kosher salt
- 2 large scallions, trimmed
- ¼ c. mango chutney, large pieces chopped
- 1/8 c. chicken broth
- ½ tsp. minced garlic
- Toasted sliced almonds, to garnish

Directions

1. Begin by cutting chicken into ½-inch thick pieces.
2. In a medium bowl, combine ground coriander, grated ginger, 2 teaspoons oil, vinegar, salt, and pepper. Mix well, then add chicken pieces to bowl to marinate. Toss chicken in bowl to coat evenly with marinade. Set aside.
3. Prepare the other ingredients. Start by thinly slicing the white parts of the scallions. Then julienne the green parts. Set aside.
4. Next, in a small bowl combine the mango chutney, chicken broth, and minced garlic. Blend well.
5. Heat the remaining 2 teaspoons of oil in a large wok (or large non-stick skillet) over medium-high heat. Add the scallion whites and julienned ginger to the wok and stir-fry for 30 seconds.
6. Next add chicken to wok and cook, stirring frequently, for 4-6 minutes or until chicken is cooked through and lightly browned.
7. Add scallion greens and mango chutney mixture. Cook, stirring constantly for an additional 2 minutes.
8. To serve, divide the chicken mixture between two dinner plates. Garnish with toasted almonds. Serve immediately.

Grilled Chicken with Corn Salsa

Yield: 2
Servings: 2 (Serving Size: 1 grilled chicken breast and corn salsa)
Total Time – Prep to Finish: 20 minutes

Ingredients

- 2 boneless, skinless chicken breast halves
- 1 tsp. fresh lemon juice
- 1 tbsp. olive oil
- 1/4 c. red onion, chopped
- ½ tsp. grated lemon peel
- 1/16 tsp. ground cumin

For the Corn Salsa:

- 1/2 c. fresh corn kernels
- 1/2 large tomato, seeded, chopped
- 2 tbsp. chopped fresh cilantro
- 1/8 to 1/4 jalapeño pepper, seeded, minced *
- 1/8 c. chopped red onion
- 1 tsp. olive oil
- 1 tsp. fresh lemon juice
- 1/8 tsp. ground cumin
- Fresh cilantro sprigs (optional)

Directions

1. Place chicken in glass baking dish.

2. In a small bowl, combine 1 tsp. lemon juice, 1 tbsp. olive oil, 1/4 c. chopped red onion, grated lemon peel, and the 1/16 tsp. ground cumin.

3. Pour the marinade ingredients over the chicken and cover the baking dish. Place in the refrigerator while preparing the grill and the salsa.

4. Preheat the grill. In a medium bowl, combine the corn, tomato, cilantro, jalapeño pepper, and the remaining red onion, olive oil, lemon juice, and ground cumin. Blend thoroughly.

5. Remove chicken from the refrigerator and marinade. Season with salt and pepper and place on the grill. Grill about 3 to 4 minute per side or until the chicken is cooked through and juices run clear.

6. Transfer each chicken breast to a dinner plate. Season with more salt and pepper, if needed. Spoon the salsa alongside the chicken and garnish the dish with fresh cilantro. Serve immediately.

Citrus Grilled Chicken Breasts

Yield: 2
Servings: 2 (Serving Size: 1 grilled chicken breast and corn salsa)
Total Time – Prep to Finish: 20 minutes

Ingredients

- 1 orange; zest and juice separated
- 1 lime
- 2 tablespoons extra virgin olive oil
- 1 teaspoon minced garlic
- 2 (6 ounce) boneless, skinless chicken breasts
- 1/4 teaspoon kosher salt
- 1/4 teaspoon black pepper (I omitted this so Mini Chef would eat it)

Instructions

6. Place the orange zest and lime into a large-sized mixing bowl; mix well. Drizzle orange juice into the bowl; mix well. Add in olive oil and garlic; mix well.

7. Place chicken in marinade and toss to coat. Cover and let chicken marinate in the refrigerator for at least 30 minutes.

8. Place grill on medium-high heat. Spray grates with high heat cooking spray. Remove chicken from marinade, sprinkle with salt and pepper, and place on preheated grill. Grill chicken, turning occasionally, for 5 - 7 minutes per side or until chicken is turned juices run clear. Remove from heat and serve alongside rice pilaf, grilled vegetables, or place on top a bed of whole-wheat pasta.

Nutrition Facts

Calories 225; **Fat** 6.8g; **Carbohydrates** 27.8g; **Fiber** 3.7g; **Sugar** 15g; **Sodium** 370mg; **Protein** 18g

Mango & Lime BBQ Turkey

Yield: 4
Servings: 4
Total Time – Prep to Finish: 20 minutes

Ingredients

- 4 boneless, skinless turkey breasts (about 1.5-lbs.)
- Juice of 2 limes
- Zest of 2 limes
- 1/2 tsp. black pepper
- 1 medium mango, chopped

Instructions

1. Combine the lime juice, lime zest, and black pepper in a sealable Ziploc bag. Add in the turkey, seal bag, and toss to coat.

2. Preheat grill to medium high and spray grates with a high heat cooking spray. Grill turkey for 5 to 7 minutes each side or until an internal temperature of about 165°F is reached.

3. While the turkey is grilling, chop up mango.

4. Remove turkey from grill and place each breast on a serving dish. Top each turkey breast with chopped mango, to garnish. Drizzle with a little lime juice, if preferred. Serve and enjoy!

Grilled Pork Chops with Strawberry-Balsamic Sauce

Yield: 6
Servings: 6
Total Time – Prep to Finish: 15 minutes

Ingredients

- 6 boneless pork loin chops
- 1/2 tsp. salt
- 1/2 tsp. pepper
- 2 cloves garlic, minced
- 1 tbsp. chopped fresh rosemary (or 1 tsp. dried)
- 2 tbsp. olive oil, divided
- 2 c. sliced fresh strawberries
- 1/4 c. balsamic vinegar
- 2 tbsp. honey

Instructions

1. Preheat grill to medium-high heat and spray grates with high heat cooking spray. Season chops with salt and pepper. Sprinkle chops with garlic and rosemary, then rub the seasonings in.

2. Place pork chops on grill and cook 2 to 3 minutes on each side or until meat is white and cooked through. Remove from heat and keep warm.

3. In a small saucepan, add strawberries, vinegar, and honey. Cook, stirring occasionally, for about 5 minutes or until sauce begins to thicken.

4. Place pork chops on serving dishes and spoon sauce over pork chops. Serve and enjoy!

Mini Pizzas with Steak and Blue Cheese

Yield: 8
Servings: 4 (Serving Size: 2 pizzas)
Total Time – Prep to Finish: 15 minutes

Ingredients

- 1-lb. ball of whole-wheat pizza dough, room temperature
- ½ c. balsamic vinegar
- Olive oil cooking spray
- 4-oz. top sirloin steak
- 1/8 tsp. sea salt
- 1/8 tsp. fresh ground black pepper
- 1 yellow onion, cut into 10-inch long slices
- 2 c. arugula
- 1 tbsp. plus 1 tsp. crumbled blue cheese (or crumbled feta cheese, if preferred)

Instructions

1. Preheat oven to 450°F. Line a baking sheet with parchment paper and set aside. Separate dough into 8 equal balls and flatten each into ¼-inch thick rounds. Arrange the dough rounds onto prepared parchment-lined baking sheet and place in oven. Let bake for 8 to 10 minutes or edges and bottom are a light golden brown. Remove from heat.

2. While the dough is in the oven, place a small saucepan over medium-high heat. Add in vinegar and bring to a boil then reduce heat to medium-low and then cook, stirring occasionally, for about 10 minutes or until vinegar is reduced by half.

3. Spray a sauté pan lightly with cooking spray. Place over medium heat. Sprinkle steak with salt and pepper to season and place in pan. Cook for about 10 minutes, turning once, or until steak has reached desired doneness. Transfer to a cutting board and tent with aluminum foil. Now, add the onion and sauté, stirring frequently, for 2 to 3 minutes, or until the onion is golden brown and translucent. Remove from heat. Slice steak against the grain. Top pizza crusts with onion, arugula, steak, and blue cheese. Drizzle each pizza with vinegar. Place back in oven and bake for 2 to 3 minutes or until cheese is bubbly. Place 2 pizzas on each serving dish and enjoy!

Leek and Lemon Linguine

Yield: 4 cups
Servings: 4 (Serving Size: 1 cup)
Total Time – Prep to Finish: 30 minutes

Ingredients

- 8-ounces whole wheat linguine or spaghetti
- 2 large lemons, plus lemon wedges for garnish
- 1 medium leek, thinly sliced and rinsed well
- 1 tbsp. extra virgin olive oil
- ½ c. flat-leaf parsley, chopped and divided
- 2 cloves garlic, crushed
- ¼ tsp. salt
- 1/8 tsp. fresh ground black pepper
- ¾ c. parmesan cheese, finely grated
- ¼ c. fresh chives, snipped and divided

Instructions

1. Place a large pot of water over medium-high to high heat. Add in 1/8 tsp. salt and 1 tsp. olive oil and bring to a boil. Cook pasta according to package directions; drain, reserving 1½ c. of pasta water. Place pasta in a large bowl, set aside and keep warm.

2. While the pasta is boiling, prepare lemons by grating 1 tbsp. zest and squeezing ¼ c. juice. Set aside. Slice leeks and pat dry. Heat oil in a large nonstick skillet over medium-high heat. Combine the leek, lemon zest, ¼ c. of the parsley, garlic, salt and pepper. Stir to blend and cook for about 6 minutes or until softened and lightly browned.

3. Add in the pasta, 1 c. of the reserved water, reserved lemon juice, remaining ¼ c. parsley to the pan. Cook, stirring constantly, for about 1 minute or until all liquid is absorbed. Add the remaining ½ c. reserved water, if necessary.

4. Remove from heat, throw out remaining garlic. Put pasta back in bowl and toss together with ½ c. parmesan and 2 tbsp. chives. Transfer 1 c. of pasta to each serving dish. Garnish each with 1 tbsp. of the remaining parmesan and 2 tsp. each of the remaining chives. Serve with lemon wedges, if desired. Perfect topped with grilled chicken breast strips.

Veggie Stir Fry

Servings: 2
Total Time – Prep to Finish: 10 minutes

Ingredients:

- 1/4 c. honey
- 1/4 c. prepared stir fry sauce
- 1/4 tsp. crushed red pepper flakes (1/4 to 1/2 teaspoon)
- 4 tsp. coconut oil or olive oil
- 2 c. small broccoli florets
- 2 c. small mushrooms
- 1 small onion, cut into wedges and separated into 1-inch strips
- 1 medium carrot, cut diagonally into 1/3 inch slices

Directions:

1. In a small bowl, combine honey, stir-fry sauce and pepper flakes, mix well and set aside.
2. In wok or large skillet, heat oil over medium-high heat; add vegetables and toss while cooking, about 2-3 minutes.
3. Add honey sauce to the vegetables. Stir to blend until all vegetables are glazed and sauce is bubbly hot, about 1 minute.

Arroz Con Pollo

Servings: 2
Total Time – Prep to Finish: 25 minutes

Ingredients:

- Olive oil cooking spray
- 2 1/2 - 3 pounds lean boneless, skinless chicken breasts, fat removed
- 1 c. chopped sweet onions
- 1 tbsp. minced garlic
- 2 tsp. cumin
- 1 c. long grain white rice
- 1 can low fat chicken broth plus water to make 2 cups of liquid
- (1) 4-ounce can chopped green chilies, with liquid
- 1/2 tsp. salt
- 1/2 tsp. ground pepper
- (1) 15-ounce can black beans, rinsed and drained
- 1 large fresh tomato, diced
- 1/3 c. chopped fresh cilantro
- 4 Lime wedges for garnish

Directions:

1. Spray very large nonstick skillet or nonstick Dutch oven or a large wok over medium high heat. Rinse chicken and pat dry. Add half the chicken to skillet and brown well, 5 minutes per side. Repeat with remaining chicken. Remove from skillet.
2. Add onions to skillet and cook, stirring until browned (add a little broth, wine or water if needed).
3. Add garlic, cumin and rice. Cook for 1 minute, stirring constantly.
4. Stir in broth and water, green chilies, salt and pepper. Bring to a boil and reduce heat.
5. Return chicken to skillet, placing it on top of the rice. Cover and simmer over medium heat until rice is tender, 10 minutes.
6. Stir in beans and tomatoes. Cover and simmer 5 minutes more. Stir in chopped cilantro.
7. Divide between two serving plates and serve with lime wedges as garnish.

Chipotle Tomato Pasta

Servings: 2
Total Time – Prep to Finish: 10 minutes

Ingredients:

- 2 cups dried whole-grain penne or ziti pasta
- (1) 12-ounce package light firm tofu, drained
- 1/4 cup oil pack sun dried tomatoes, drained well
- 1/4 cup fat free vegetable broth
- 1 teaspoon dried oregano
- 1 teaspoon dried basil
- 1 or 2 chipotle peppers in adobo sauce
- 1/2 teaspoon salt
- 2 cloves garlic, minced
- 1/2 tbsp. fresh basil leaves, shredded (to garnish)
- Parmesan cheese, freshly grated, to garnish (optional)

Directions:

1. In a blender container, combine tofu, tomatoes, both, oregano, basil, peppers, garlic and salt. Cover and blend until nearly smooth.
2. Transfer to a bowl and toss with hot cooked pasta prepared according to package direction.
3. Divide and transfer to two dinner plates. Garnish with shredded basil leaves and Parmesan cheese if desired. Serve immediately.

Greek Grilled Chicken Kabobs:

Servings: 2 (serving size: 3 kabobs)
Total Time – Prep to Finish: 20 minutes

Ingredients:

- 8 oz. (1 container) Greek yogurt, plain
- 1/3 c. crumbled feta cheese
- 1/2 tsp. lemon zest
- 2 tbsp. fresh lemon juice
- 2 tsp. dried oregano
- 1/2 tsp. salt
- 1/4 tsp. ground black pepper
- 1/4 tsp. dried parsley flakes
- 1/4 tsp. crushed dried rosemary
- 1-lb. boneless, skinless chicken breast halves, cut into 1-inch pieces.
- 1 large red sweet onion, cut into wedges
- 1 large green bell pepper, cut into 1 1/2-inch pieces
- 1 c. pineapple chunks (if using canned pineapple, make sure to get the canned pineapple in water or fruit juice, not syrup)
- 6 metal skewers

Directions:

1. In a large, shallow baking dish, mix together the plain Greek yogurt, feta cheese, lemon zest, lemon juice, oregano, salt, pepper, parsley flakes, and rosemary.

2. Place the chicken in the dish, and turn to coat. Cover, and place in the refrigerator to marinate 10 minutes. (You can also prepare the chicken ahead of time for a longer marinating time). While the chicken is marinating, wash and prepare the vegetables. Cut the red sweet onion into wedges; cut the green bell pepper into 1 1/2-inch pieces. If the pineapple is not already cut into chunks, do so now.

3. Preheat the grill for high heat. Using high-heat cooking spray, coat the grill grates to prevent the kabobs from sticking to the grates.

4. Remove the marinated chicken from the refrigerator. Thread the chicken, onion wedges, green bell pepper pieces, and pineapple chunks alternately onto the skewers. Try to get at least 3 to 4 pieces of chicken per skewer. Discard the remaining yogurt marinade mixture.

5. Place the skewers onto the grates and grill until the chicken is no longer pink and juices run clear, about 7-8 minutes. Remove the skewers from the grill and transfer 3 skewers onto each serving dish. Serve immediately.

Grilled Chicken Fajitas

Yield: 2 wraps
Servings: 2 (Serving Size: 1 wrap)
Total Time – Prep to Finish: 10 minutes

Ingredients:

- 2 c. fully-cooked grilled chicken breast strips
- 1 red bell pepper but into 1/4-inch strips
- 1 yellow bell pepper but into 1/4-inch strips
- 1 onion, sliced
- 1/2 tbsp. dried oregano
- 1/2 tbsp. chili powder
- 1/2 tbsp. cumin
- 1/2 tbsp. coriander
- 1 1/2 garlic cloves, chopped
- juice of 1 lemon
- 1 tbsp coconut oil
- 4 whole wheat (fajita size) tortilla
- 1/2 c. diced tomatoes, to garnish (opt.)
- 1/2 c. sliced avocado, to garnish (opt.)
- 1/4 c. salsa, to garnish (opt.)

Directions

1. In a medium size bowl, combine the grilled chicken strips, sliced bell pepper, sliced onions, spices, chopped garlic, and lemon juice. Mix well.

2. Place a large non-stick skillet over medium heat. Add the coconut oil to the skillet. Transfer the bowl of mixed ingredients to the skillet and cook for about 5 to 7 minutes or until the grilled chicken is heated through, the peppers are tender, the onion translucent, and the garlic fragrant.

3. Warm and place 2 whole-wheat tortillas onto two separate dinner plates. Divide the fajita mixture among the two plates. Scoop the fajita mixture onto the tortillas. If desired, garnish the fajitas with diced tomato, sliced avocado, and/or salsa. Serve immediately.

Black Bean Cakes

Servings: 2
Total Time – Prep to Finish: 15 minutes

Ingredients:

- 1/2 (16-ounce) can black beans, drained and well rinsed
- 1/4 green bell pepper, finely chopped
- 1/4 onion, finely chopped
- 1 1/2 cloves garlic, peeled and very finely chopped
- 1 large egg
- 1/2 tbsp. chili powder
- 1/2 tbsp. cumin
- 1/2 tsp. hot sauce
- 1/2 c. bread crumbs
- 1 tsp. extra-virgin olive oil
- 2 pieces of Bibb Lettuce

Directions:

1) Preheat oven to 375° F. Using the olive oil, lightly grease a baking sheet and then line it with aluminum foil.

2) In a medium bowl, use a fork to mash the black beans. Next, add the finely chopped bell pepper, onion, and garlic and stir until mixed thoroughly.

3) Crack the egg into a small bowl and whisk. Now stir in the chili powder, cumin, and hot sauce. Transfer the egg mixture to the bowl with the mashed beans and slowly stir in the egg mixture.

4) Add the bread crumbs to the mixture and blend well until the mixture is sticky and holds together. Divide mixture into 2 patties. Place the patties in the freezer and chill for 5 minutes.

5) Transfer the patties to the baking sheet, place in preheated oven and bake about 7 to 8 minutes or until the patties are crispy on each side.

6) Place a piece of Bibb lettuce on two separate dinner plates. Top each bed of lettuce with a patty. Serve immediately.

Lemon Herb Chicken

Yield: 2
Servings: 2 (Serving Size: 1 half breast)
Total Time – Prep to Finish: 15 minutes

Ingredients

- 2 boneless, skinless chicken breast halves
- Juice of 1 lemon
- Dash of sea salt, to taste
- Dash of lemon pepper seasoning, to taste
- 1 generous pinch dried oregano
- 2 sprigs fresh parsley, for garnish
- Olive oil cooking spray

Directions

1. Cut lemon in half and squeeze the juice from 1/2 of the lemon onto the chicken breast halves. Season the chicken with a dash of sea salt, to taste. Let sit while you spray a non-stick skillet with cooking spray and place over medium-low heat.

2. When hot, transfer chicken breast halves to the skillet. As you sauté the chicken, begin adding juice from the other 1/2 of the lemon, along with the oregano, lemon pepper seasoning, and additional sea salt to taste. Sauté for 5 to 10 minutes each side, or until chicken is cooked through and juices run clear. Transfer the chicken breast halves to two separate dinner plates. Garnish the chicken with a sprig or two of parsley. Serve immediately.

Mini Meatloaf

Yield: 6 mini meatloaf's
Servings: 3 (Serving Size: 1 wrap)
Total Time – Prep to Finish: 10 minutes

Ingredients

- 1 lbs. organic ground turkey
- 1 1/2 tsp. sea salt
- 1 tsp. pepper
- 1 tsp. paprika
- 1 tbsp. fresh organic parsley, finely chopped
- 1 organic onion, chopped
- 1 cage-free organic egg (optional)

Directions

1. In a medium-sized bowl, combine all ingredients and mix together thoroughly until well blended.

2. Roll the ground turkey mixture into 6 equal balls and then flatten the balls only slightly.

3. Place a large non-stick skillet, sprayed with olive oil cooking spray, over medium heat. Place the mini meatloaf's in the skillet, two at a time, and cook about 2 to 3 minutes on each side, turning only once. The mini meatloaf's are done when the meat is cooked through and each side is a light golden brown.

4. Divide the mini meatloaf's among two separate dinner plates. Serve immediately.

Turkey-Stuffed Zucchini

Yield: 2 wraps
Servings: 2 (Serving Size: 1 wrap)
Total Time – Prep to Finish: 10 minutes

Ingredients

- 1 zucchini about 6-inches long, sliced in half lengthwise.
- 3 tbsp. extra-virgin olive oil
- 1/4 c. chopped onion
- 1 ½ cloves garlic, minced
- ¼ c. chopped mushrooms
- 1 tbsp. dry white wine
- ¼ lb. (6oz.) ground turkey
- 1 medium tomato, diced
- 1½ tbsp. fresh chopped basil
- ½ tsp. chopped rosemary
- 1 large egg, beaten
- 1 tsp. sea salt
- 1 tsp. fresh ground black pepper
- Grated Parmesan cheese, to garnish (opt.)

Directions

1. Cut the zucchini in half, lengthwise, and scoop out the insides until you are left with 2 shells approximately 1/4 -inch thick. Reserve half of the insides to be used later and discard the leftover insides.

2. In a large skillet over medium-high heat, heat 2 tbsp. of olive oil. When hot, begin sautéing the onion and garlic until they become soft and fragrant. Toss in mushrooms and the reserved zucchini insides. Sauté for 2 more minutes.

3. In another skillet, heat 1 tbsp. olive oil over medium-high heat. Add ground turkey to the pan and lightly brown, stirring occasionally, to ensure every side gets browned, about 6 minutes. Add onion and mushroom mixture to the ground turkey and stir to blend. Stir in wine. Stir in tomato, basil, rosemary and cook for 1 minute. Drain any fat and remove from heat. Set aside.

4. When mixture has cooled, add egg, milk, salt, pepper, and sprinkle in a bit of cheese. Fill zucchini shells with mixture and place zucchini halves in a baking pan filed with ¼-inch of water. Bake at 375°F for 10 to 12 minutes or until golden brown. To serve, transfer to plate and serve hot.

Greek Meatballs with Greek Yogurt Dip

Yield: 10 meatballs
Servings: 2 (Serving Size: 5 meatballs; ½ c. dip)
Total Time – Prep to Finish: 15 minutes

Ingredients

- 1 tbsp. extra-virgin olive oil
- ½ clove garlic, minced
- ½ jalapeno, seeded and minced
- 1 medium shallot, minced
- ½ lb. (8 oz.) ground lamb
- 2 oz. salt pork, ground or finely minced
- Zest of ½ an orange (1 tbsp. zest)
- 1 tbsp. chopped mint
- Freshly ground pepper
- 1 cup Greek yogurt for dipping

Directions

1. Heat the olive oil in a small pan over medium heat. When the oil is hot, add the garlic, jalapeno, and shallot. Sauté for 1 minute and then set aside to cool.

2. In a medium-size bowl, crumble up ground lamb. Sprinkle the salt pork, orange zest, and chopped mint over ground lamb. Add the cooled garlic mixture to ground lamb. Work the ingredients into the lamb until blended.

3. Form the ground lamb mixture into 1¼-inch balls and transfer to a baking sheet or plate.

4. Heat a cast iron pan over medium to medium-high heat, Once hot, transfer meatballs to pan and brown on all sides for about 8-10 minutes or until cooked through.

5. To serve, transfer to serving to two serving dishes. Serve the meatballs with 1/2 c. Greek plain yogurt for dipping. Serve warm.

Seared Ahi Tuna

Yield: 2 (4 oz.) tuna steaks
Servings: 2 (Serving Size: 1 tuna steak)
Total Time – Prep to Finish: 15 to 20 minutes

Ingredients

- 2 (4-ounces each) ahi tuna steaks (3/4-inch thick)
- 2 tbsp. dark sesame oil
- 2 tbsp. soy sauce
- 1 tbsp. of grated fresh ginger
- 1 clove garlic, minced
- 1 green onion (scallion) thinly sliced, reserve a few slices for garnish
- 1 tsp. lime juice

Directions

1. Begin by preparing the marinade. In a small bowl, whisk together the sesame oil, soy sauce, fresh ginger, minced garlic, green onion, and lime juice. Mix well.

2. Place tuna steaks into a sealable Ziploc freezer bag and pour marinade over the top of the tuna. Seal bag and shake or massage with hands to coat tuna steaks well with marinade. Place bag in bowl, in case of breaks, and place tuna in refrigerator to marinate for at least 10 minutes.

3. Place a large non-stick skillet over medium-high to high heat. Let pan heat for 2 minutes, when hot, remove tuna steaks from the marinade and lay them in the pan to sear for 1-1½ minutes on each side.

4. Remove tuna steaks from pan and cut into ¼-inch thick slices. Garnish with a sprinkle of sliced green onion. Serve immediately.

Spicy Turkey & Avocado Burgers

Yield: 2 wraps
Servings: 2 (Serving Size: 1 wrap)
Total Time – Prep to Finish: 10 minutes

Ingredients

- 1/2 lb. ground turkey
- 1/8 c. almond flour (Use only enough so that the turkey is not too soft enough to work with)
- 1/2 tbsp. garlic powder
- 1/2 tbsp. red pepper flakes
- 1/4 tbsp. dried minced onion
- sea salt, to taste
- black pepper, to taste
- 2 to 4 beds of Bibb lettuce (or lettuce of choice)
- 1 avocado, peeled and cut into chunks to make 1/2 cup.

Directions

1) In a medium sized, shallow bowl combine all ingredients until blended together thoroughly. Divide the ground turkey mixture and form into 2 patties.

2) Grill on each side for 3 to 5 minutes, or until cooked through. Sprinkle with salt and pepper, to taste.

3) Place a bed of Bibb lettuce onto two plates. Place a turkey burger onto each bed of lettuce.

4) Top each burger with 1/4 c. of avocado pieces.

5) Serve immediately.

Herbes de Provence - Crusted Salmon w/ Citrus-Herb Sauce

Yield: 2 filets
Servings: 2 (Serving Size: 1 filet)
Total Time – Prep to Finish: 10 minutes

Ingredients

- 2 (6-oz.) salmon filets
- 1/2 c. orange juice (about 1 orange)
- 1/2 tbsp. fresh thyme, chopped
- 1/2 tbsp. dried oregano
- Zest of 1 lemon
- 1 tsp. sea salt
- 1/2 tsp. fresh ground black pepper
- 1/2 tsp. Herbes de Provence
- 1/2 pound asparagus, tough ends removed
- 1 tbsp. extra-virgin olive oil
- sea salt and black pepper, to taste

Directions

1. Begin by preparing the citrus-herb sauce: Whisk together in a small shallow bowl, the orange juice, thyme, and oregano. Place half of the sauce in a plastic zip-lock bag. Set the remaining sauce aside to be used later.

2. Add the salmon to the zip-lock bag. Seal the bag and set aside to let marinate for 5 minutes at room temperature.

3. Transfer the remaining sauce to a sauté pan and place over medium heat. Bring the sauce to a light boil, then reduce heat and let simmer for a few minutes until the sauce reduces slightly.

4. Heat the grill and cut out 2 squares of aluminum foil. Place a salmon filet onto the center of each piece of foil. In a small bowl, combine the zest, tsp. of salt and 1/2 tsp. of black pepper as well as Herbes de Provence. Drizzle the lemon zest mixture over each salmon filet. Wrap the salmon in the foil. On a third piece of foil, place the asparagus spears. Drizzle the spears with olive oil and sprinkle with salt and pepper to season. Place the salmon and asparagus on the grill and cook for 8 to 10 minutes.

5. Remove from grill and place a salmon filet on each plate. Divide the asparagus spears and arrange them on each plate next to the salmon filets. Drizzle the remaining citrus-herb sauce over the salmon and asparagus on each plate and serve immediately.

Pineapple & Grilled Chicken Stir-Fry

Servings: 2 (Serving Size: 4 oz. chicken and half of pineapple mixture)
Total Time – Prep to Finish: 10 minutes

Ingredients

- 8-ounces of fully cooked grilled chicken breast strips, cut into chunks.
- 3/4 to 1 can pineapple chunks
- 1 clove garlic, minced
- 1 tbsp. fresh ginger root, minced
- 1/2 to 1 tbsp. extra virgin olive oil (may instead use coconut oil or other oil of choice)
- 1/4 green bell pepper, cut into strips or chunks
- 1/4 red bell pepper, cut into strips or chunks
- 1/4 onion, sliced or cut into chunks
- 1½ scallions, sliced
- 1 c. broccoli (optional)
- 1/4 c. pineapple juice (reserved from can of pineapple chunks)
- 2 tbsp. coconut oil
- 1/2 tbsp. sesame oil
- 1/2 tbsp. arrowroot starch
- 2 tsp. honey
- 1 tsp. coconut palm sugar (opt,)

Directions

1. Begin by draining the pineapple chunks, reserving 1/4 cup of the pineapple juice for the sauce.

2. Heat the olive oil in a large wok over medium heat. Add the grilled chicken pieces, minced garlic, and the minced ginger root. Stir-fry for 2 minutes.

3. Add the pineapple chunks, onion, red and green pepper, and broccoli. Cover the wok and allow the contents to steam for about 2 to 3 minutes or until tender-crisp.

4. Prepare the sauce: In a small bowl combine the reserved pineapple juice, coconut oil, sesame oil, starch, honey, and coconut palm sugar (opt.) and whisk together until well blended.

5. Drizzle the sauce over the contents in the wok. Add the scallions. Toss until the contents are coated with the sauce and the sauce begins to thicken. Divide the stir-fry among two dinner plates and serve immediately.

Shrimp in Coconut Sauce

Servings: 2 (Serving Size: 10 shrimp ½ c. coconut sauce)
Total Time – Prep to Finish: 10 minutes

Ingredients

- 20 cocktail shrimp
- 8 oz. mini bella mushrooms, sliced
- 1 - 2 tbsp. coconut oil.
- 1 c. sweet peas
- 1 c. canned coconut milk
- 1 tsp. ground coriander
- 1/2 tsp. ground ginger
- 1/2 tsp. ground cinnamon
- 1/2 tsp. turmeric
- Dash of sea salt and pepper, to taste
- shredded coconut, to garnish (opt.)

Directions

1. Remove tails from the shrimp.
2. Heat the coconut oil in a sauté pan over medium heat. Add the mushrooms and sauté for 1 to 2 minutes.
3. Add the coconut milk, peas, and spices to the pan, stir to blend well. Reduce heat and let simmer 5 to 8 minutes or until the sauce begins to thicken.
4. Add the shrimp and continue to cook an additional 3 to 5 minutes or until the shrimp is heated through. Divide between two plates. Drizzle any remaining sauce left behind in the pan over each dish. Serve immediately.

Slow-Cooker Vegetarian Chili

Yield: 7 c.

Servings: 6 (Serving Size: 1 ½ c. chili)

Total Time – Prep to Finish: 6 hours 15 minutes

Ingredients:

- 1 (28-ounce) can diced tomatoes
- 4 cups reduced-sodium vegetable broth
- 1 (15-ounce) can black beans, rinsed and drained
- 1 (15-ounce) can white (cannellini) beans, rinsed and drained
- 1 (15-ounce) can red kidney beans, rinsed and drained
- 1 c. frozen baby lima beans or regular lima beans
- 1 c. chopped onion
- 1 green bell pepper, seeded and chopped
- 2 cloves garlic, minced
- 1 tbsp. minced pickled jalapeno (from can or jar)
- 2 tbsp. chili powder
- 2 tbsp. dried Mexican oregano or regular oregano
- 2 tsp. ground cumin
- 1 tsp. ground coriander
- 1 to 2 teaspoons hot sauce
- 1/3 c. couscous
- 1/2 c. shredded Monterey jack cheese
- 1/3 c. chopped fresh cilantro leaves
- Salt and freshly ground black pepper

Instructions:

1. In a slow cooker, combine all ingredients but the couscous, shredded cheese, cilantro and salt and pepper. Cover and cook on LOW for 6 to 8 hours or on HIGH for 3 to 4 hours.

2. Five to 10 minutes before serving (depending on temperature of slow cooker) add couscous, cover and cook, until couscous is tender. Season, to taste, with salt and black pepper.

3. Just before serving, top each serving with shredded cheese and cilantro.

Fettuccini Alfredo with Zucchini Ribbons

Servings: 2
Total Time – Prep to Finish: 30 minutes

Ingredients

- 2 tbsp. olive oil
- 2 cloves garlic, minced
- 2 medium zucchini (about 8 ounces each)
- 12 oz. whole wheat Fettuccini pasta, preferably whole wheat
- 1 tbsp. all-purpose flour
- 1 c. cold 1% low-fat milk
- 1/2 c. evaporated skim milk (not condensed milk)
- 1/2 tsp. salt, plus more to taste
- 3/4 c. freshly grated Parmesan cheese
- 1/4 c. finely chopped fresh parsley leaves

Directions

1. Slice the ends off the zucchini and discard. Using a mandolin or carefully with a sharp knife slice the zucchini lengthwise into very thin slices. Stack the slices and cut with a knife lengthwise into 1/4 inch-thick ribbons.

2. Heat 1 tablespoon of the oil in large non-stick skillet over a medium heat. Add 1 clove of the garlic and cook for 30 seconds. Add the zucchini ribbons, cover and cook until the zucchini is tender, stirring occasionally, about 6 minutes. Transfer the zucchini to a bowl.

3. Cook the pasta al dente according to the directions on the package. Ladle out a half cup of the pasta water and set aside. Drain the pasta and return it to the pasta pot.

4. Meanwhile, make the sauce. Stir the flour into the low-fat milk until it is completely dissolved. Put the remaining tablespoon of olive oil in the skillet and heat over a medium-high heat. Add the remaining clove of garlic and cook for 30 seconds. Add the flour-milk mixture and cook until the mixture begins to boil, stirring constantly. Reduce heat to low and cook, stirring, for 2 minutes more. Add the evaporated milk, salt and the cheese and cook, stirring, until the cheese is melted, about 1 minute. Season with additional salt to taste.

5. Add the sauce, the zucchini and 3 tablespoons of the parsley to the pasta in the pot and toss to combine. Add a little of the reserved pasta water as necessary to loosen. To serve, place 2 cups of the pasta mixture on each plate and garnish with remaining parsley.

Kale & Portobello Lasagna

Yield: 12 c.
Servings: 8 (Serving Size: 1 ½ c.)
Total Time – Prep to Finish: 1 hour 50 minutes

Ingredients

- 1 c. coarsely chopped drained jarred roasted red peppers
- 1/2 tsp. dried oregano
- One 28-ounce can no-salt-added whole plum tomatoes
- Kosher salt and freshly ground black pepper
- 1/4 tsp. granulated sugar
- 1 1/2 c. grated part-skim mozzarella cheese
- 2 large egg whites
- One 15-ounce container part-skim ricotta cheese
- 1 tbsp. olive oil
- 4 Portobello mushrooms, stems discarded, caps sliced 1/4-inch thick
- 1 small bunch kale, stems discarded, leaves coarsely chopped
- 1/4 tsp. crushed red pepper flakes
- 2 cloves garlic, thinly sliced
- Nonstick cooking spray
- 9 sheets no-boil lasagna noodles, such as Barilla
- 2 tablespoons coarsely chopped fresh parsley

Directions

1. Preheat the oven to 350 degrees F. Puree the peppers, oregano, tomatoes, 1/4 teaspoon salt, 1/4 teaspoon pepper and the sugar in a food processor or blender until smooth and set aside. Mix 1 cup of the mozzarella cheese with the egg whites and ricotta cheese in a medium bowl.

2. Heat the oil in a large nonstick skillet set over medium-high heat. Add the sliced mushrooms and cook, stirring, until they have released their liquid and are tender, about 10 minutes. Stir in the kale, in batches, and as it wilts add the pepper flakes, garlic and 1/4 teaspoon salt and continue to cook until the kale is wilted and bright green, an additional 5 minutes.

3. Mist a 9-by-13-inch baking dish with nonstick cooking spray. Spread 3/4 cup of the sauce in the bottom of the dish. Top with 3 noodles, 1/2 of the ricotta mixture and 1/2 of the mushroom mixture. Repeat layers with sauce, noodles and remaining ricotta and mushrooms. Top with remaining noodles and sauce. Cover with aluminum foil and bake until the noodles are tender and the sauce is bubbling around the edges of the pan, about 50 minutes.

4. Uncover, sprinkle with the remaining 1/2 cup grated mozzarella and continue to bake until melted, about 5 minutes. Let stand 15 minutes, sprinkle with parsley and serve.

Parmesan & Yogurt Crusted Salmon

Yield: 4 filets
Servings: 4 (Serving Size: 1 filet)
Total Time – Prep to Finish: 20 minutes

Ingredients

- 1½ -pounds (four 6-ounce) salmon fillets (skinned)
- 2½ tbsp. plain Greek yogurt
- 2½ tbsp. mayonnaise
- 2 tbsp. grated Parmesan cheese
- 2 tbsp. fresh chives, snipped (substitute finely chopped green onion, if preferred)
- ½ tsp. Worcestershire sauce
- freshly ground pepper, to taste

Directions

1. First, preheat oven to 450°F.

2. In a small bowl, combine plain yogurt, mayonnaise, Parmesan cheese, chives (or green onions), Worcestershire sauce, and a pinch of black pepper, to taste. Blend thoroughly.

3. Lightly grease a baking sheet and arrange the salmon filets on the baking sheet.

4. Coat the top of each fillet with the parmesan-yogurt mixture and place on the top rack of a preheated oven. Bake the salmon for approximately 7 to10 minutes or until the salmon is just cooked through and the parmesan-yogurt crust is a light golden brown.

5. Remove fillets from oven and serve immediately.

Honey-Mustard Salmon with Grilled Asparagus

Yield: 4 salmon filets
Servings: 4 (Serving Size: 1 salmon filet; ¼ -lb. asparagus)
Total Time – Prep to Finish: 25 minutes

Ingredients

- 4 salmon fillets (6 oz. each)
- sea salt, to taste
- fresh ground black pepper, to taste
- 2 tbsp. Dijon mustard
- 2 tbsp. honey
- 1/2 tsp. horseradish
- 1-pound asparagus, trimmed
- 2 tbsp. extra virgin olive oil

Directions

1. Preheat oven to medium low.

2. First, season salmon filets with sea salt and black pepper.

3. In a small-sized mixing bowl, whisk together the mustard, horseradish, and 1 tbsp. of olive oil until well-blended and brush all over filets.

4. Take trimmed asparagus and coat it with the remaining olive oil and lightly season with sea salt and black pepper, to taste.

5. Cut (8) 12 x 12-inch pieces of aluminum foil and double them up so that you are left with 4 pieces of double-thickness foil. Place one salmon filet and equal amounts of asparagus along each side of the salmon then fold and seal.

6. Place the four foil-wrapped filets on the grill and cook covered for about 15 minutes or until the asparagus is tender-crisp and the salmon flakes easily. Unwrap each foil and place onto 4 serving dishes.

Slow Cooker Cilantro-Lime Chicken Tacos

Yield: 8 tacos
Servings: 4 (Serving Size: 2 tacos)
Total Time – Prep to Finish: 4 hours 5 minutes

Ingredients

- 1- to 2-pounds boneless skinless chicken breasts
- juice of 2 limes
- ½ c. fresh cilantro, chopped
- 1 packet of taco seasoning
- 1 tsp. dried onions
- ½ c. water
- 8 whole-wheat or flour tortillas (soft-taco size)
- 1 to 2 limes, wedged

Directions

1. Place chicken breasts into the slow cooker

2. In a small-mixing bowl combine lime juice, chopped cilantro, taco seasoning, dried onions, and water. Stir until well-blended.

3. Pour cilantro-lime mixture over chicken breasts in slow cooker.

4. Cook contents on LOW heat for 6 to 8 hours or until chicken is cooked through. If in a hurry, cook on HIGH for 4 hours.

5. Remove chicken from slow cooker and using a fork, shred the chicken breasts.

6. Spoon the shredded cilantro-lime chicken into tortillas and top with shredded cheese, lettuce, tomato, salsa, sour cream or any other preferred toppings. Serve with a wedge or two of fresh lime.

Zesty Orange Chicken Stir-Fry

Servings: 4 to 6 (Serving Size: 1 to 1½ c.)
Total Time – Prep to Finish: 30 minutes

Ingredients

Sauce

- ½ c. orange juice
- 2 tbsp. soy sauce
- 2 tbsp. rice vinegar
- 1 tbsp. oyster sauce
- 1 tbsp. orange zest
- 2 large cloves garlic
- 1 tsp. minced ginger
- Optional sweetener like sugar, honey, agave, etc.

Stir-Fry

- 1-pound chicken tender, cut into cubes
- salt and pepper, to taste
- 3 tbsp. corn starch
- 4 c. chopped vegetables such as broccoli, carrots, celery, mushroom, snap peas, etc.
- extra-virgin olive oil
- ½ c. medium yellow onion, chopped

Directions

1. To begin, heat wok over medium-high heat.

2. Place sauce ingredients in a blender and process until smooth. Add sweeter of choice, if preferred.

3. Place sauce in wok and heat for 5 minutes then place in a heat-safe bowl.

4. Clean skillet. Season chicken with salt and pepper. Massage the cornstarch into the chicken with your hands.

5. Heat 1 tbsp. of olive oil in skillet over medium-high heat. Cook the onion and chicken in skillet for 3 to 4 minutes or until chicken is cooked through. Next, add vegetables and stir-fry together.

6. Slowly add a few tbsp. of sauce to skillet while stirring chicken and vegetables.

7. Continue to slowly add sauce a few tbsp. at a time, allowing 15 seconds between each addition of sauce.

8. To serve, spoon stir-fry over a bowl of hot rice and enjoy.

~ *Snack/Dessert Recipes* ~

Cinnamon Crunch Granola

Yield: 1 c. granola
Servings: 2 (Serving Size: ½ c. granola)
Total Time – Prep to Finish: 10 minutes

Ingredients

- 1/2 c. almonds
- 1/2 c. walnuts
- 1 c. shredded coconut, unsweetened
- 1 tbsp. coconut oil
- 1 tsp. cinnamon
- 1 tbsp. maple syrup
- pinch of sea salt, to taste

Directions

1. Melt the coconut oil in a pan over medium heat,. Add the almonds and walnuts and toss for 1 minute.

2. Add the cinnamon, maple syrup, shredded coconut, and a pinch of sea salt. Blend thoroughly.

3. Sauté ingredients for 2 to 4 minutes or until coconut flakes are slightly browned. Let cool, if desired or eat hot. Serve by itself or with yogurt.

Pistachio-Pineapple Snack Plate

Yield: 2 snack plates
Servings: 2 (Serving Size: 25 pistachios; ¼ c. dried pineapple)
Total Time – Prep to Finish: 3 minutes

Ingredients

- 50 pistachios
- ½ c. dried pineapple, chopped into pieces

Directions

1. On a snack plate, arrange a small bowl of 25 pistachios, alongside a 1/4 c. of dried pineapple slices or pieces.

2. Repeat process for second serving and serve immediately.

Peanut-Raisin Snack Plate

Yield: 2 snack plates
Servings: 2 (Serving Size: 20 peanuts; 1/8 c. raisins)
Total Time – Prep to Finish: 3 minutes

Ingredients

- 40 peanuts
- ¼ c. raisins

Directions

1. On a snack plate, arrange a small bowl of 20 peanuts, alongside a 1/8 c. of raisins.

2. Repeat process for second serving and serve immediately.

Apricot & Almond Snack Plate

Yield: 2 snack plates
Servings: 2 (Serving Size: 15 almonds; ¼ c. dried apricots)
Total Time – Prep to Finish: 3 minutes

Ingredients

- 30 almonds
- 1/2 c. dried apricots

Directions

1. On a snack plate, arrange a small bowl of 15 pistachios, alongside a 1/4 c. of dried apricots.

2. Repeat process for second serving and serve immediately.

Hazelnut & Cherries Snack Plate

Yield: 2 snack plates
Servings: 2 (Serving Size: 15 hazelnuts; ¼ c. cherries)
Total Time – Prep to Finish: 3 minutes

Ingredients

- 30 hazelnuts
- ½ c. cherries of choice

Directions

1. On a snack plate, arrange a small bowl of 15 hazelnuts, alongside a 1/4 c. of cherries.
2. Repeat process for second serving and serve immediately.

Apple-Spiced Kale Chips

Yield: 4
Servings: 4
Total Time – Prep to Finish: 10 minutes

Ingredients

- 2 tbsp. apple cider vinegar
- 1 tsp. sea salt
- 1 tbsp. extra virgin olive oil
- 6 c. fresh kale, chopped

Instructions

1. Preheat oven to 350°F.

2. Wash kale, pat dry, and then chop.

3. Place kale in a sealable freezer bag. Add olive oil, seal bag, and toss until kale is evenly coated in oil.

4. Open bag and pour in vinegar. Seal bag and toss again to coat kale.

5. Place kale on sturdy baking sheet and place in preheated oven for 10 minutes. Remove from oven and toss gently to move kale around.

6. Place kale back in oven and bake for an addition 8 to 12 minutes or until the desired crispiness is reached. NOTE: if kale is still soft, but browning too quickly, reduce heat to 325°F and keep a watchful eye.

7. Remove kale chips from oven and sprinkle with sea salt, to taste. Serve hot or wait until cool. Store remaining kale chips in airtight container.

Watermelon-Lime Salsa

Yield: 2 cups
Servings: 4 (Serving Size: ½ c.)
Total Time – Prep to Finish: 20 minutes

Ingredients

- 1 to 1½ c. watermelon, finely diced
- 1/2 jalapeno pepper, seeded and minced
- 1 1/3 tbsp. fresh cilantro, chopped
- 1 tbsp. lime juice
- 1 tbsp. red onion, minced
- Sea salt, to taste
- 20 blue corn tortilla chips (or pita wedges, if preferred)

Instructions

1. In a medium-sized mixing bowl, combine watermelon, minced jalapeno, cilantro, lime juice, and red onion. Stir until well blended.

2. Sprinkle with sea salt, to taste.

3. Place 1/2 c. salsa and enjoy. Try alongside tortilla or kale chips.

4. Any remaining salsa can be covered and stored in the refrigerator for up to 24-hours.

Cheerios Trail Mix

Yield: 3 cups
Servings: 6 (Serving Size: ½ c.)
Total Time – Prep to Finish: 10 minutes

Ingredients

- 3 c. Cheerios cereal
- ¾ c. pumpkin seeds (or sunflower seeds, if preferred)
- ½ c. raisins
- ½ c. semisweet min chocolate chips

Instructions

1. In a sealable freezer bag, combine Cheerios, pumpkin seeds, raisins, and mini chocolate chips.
2. Seal bag and shake to blend.
3. Serving size: 1/2 c. trail mix. Remaining trail mix can be stored in airtight container for up to one month.

Blackberry Almond Parfait

Yield: 4 parfaits
Servings: 4 (Serving Size: 1 parfait)
Total Time – Prep to Finish: 10 minutes

Ingredients

- 4 c. vanilla-flavored Greek yogurt (or plain)
- 2 c. blackberries
- 2 tsp. vanilla extract
- 4 tsp. ground flaxseeds
- 4 tbsp. sliced almonds
- 8 tbsp. granola of choice

Instructions

1. Combine yogurt, vanilla and flaxseeds in a bowl. Blend Well. Spoon ½ c. of the yogurt mixture into two parfait dishes.

2. Layer each parfait dish with ¼ c. blackberries and ½ tbsp. almonds.

3. Next, top each dish with another 1/2 c. yogurt, followed by ¼ c. blackberries, ½ tbsp. almonds, and finally 2 tbsp. granola. Serve immediately.

Greek Yogurt Bowl w/ Strawberries & Cinnamon Maple Crunch Topping

Yield: 4 yogurt bowls
Servings: 4 (Serving Size: 1 yogurt bowl)
Total Time – Prep to Finish: 30 minutes

Ingredients

- 2 cantaloupes, cut in half
- 1 c. plain or vanilla low-fat yogurt (use Greek yogurt, if preferred)
- ½ c. fresh strawberries
- 1 c. almonds
- 1 c. walnuts
- 2 c. shredded coconut, unsweetened
- 1-2 tbsp. coconut oil
- 2 tsp. cinnamon
- 2 tbsp. maple syrup
- pinch of sea salt, to taste

Instructions

1. Cut cantaloupe in half, using spoon scrape out insides to form 2 bowls.

2. *Prepare maple crunch topping*: Melt the coconut oil in a pan over medium heat. Add the almonds and walnuts and toss for 1 minute. Add the cinnamon, maple syrup, shredded coconut, and a pinch of sea salt. Blend thoroughly. Sauté ingredients for 2 to 4 minutes or until coconut flakes are slightly browned. Let cool.

3. Place ¼ c. yogurt into each "bowl" and top yogurt with ¼ c. topping and 1/8 c. strawberries. Serve and enjoy!

Mini Caramel Cheesecakes

Yield: 6 cheesecakes
Servings: 6 (Serving Size: 1 cheesecake)
Total Time – Prep to Finish: 45 minutes

Ingredients

- 1/3 c. sucanat
- 2 tbsp. water
- 6-oz. light cream cheese
- 2 large eggs
- ¼ c. nonfat plain Greek yogurt
- 1/3 c. organic evaporated cane juice
- 6 (4-oz.) ramekins

Instructions

1. Preheat oven to 350°F. Place a small saucepan over medium-high heat and add in the sucanat and 2 tbsp. water. Bring to a boil. Continue boiling, stirring constantly and gently, for an additional 30 – 45 seconds or until slightly thickened. Divide evenly among the 6 ramekins.

2. In a food processor or blender, combine cream cheese, eggs, yogurt, and cane juice. Pulse until smooth. Spoon evenly among the 6 ramekins over the top of the sucanat mixture.

3. Set ramekins inside 9 x 13-inch baking pan and fill pan halfway with warm water. Place in oven and bake for 20 to 30 minutes or until a tip (just the tip!) of a knife inserted in the center of a cheesecake comes out clean. Turn oven off and let cheesecakes cool to room temperature inside of the oven (to prevent cracking).

4. When ready to serve, run a knife around the edges of the ramekins and place ramekins inside a pan of very hot water in order to loosen the caramel. Let the ramekins sit in the water for 5 minutes, then remove from water and invert each ramekin onto a serving dish. Serve immediately.

Cream Cheese S'mores

Yield: 4 smores
Servings: 4 (Serving Size: 1 smore)
Total Time – Prep to Finish: 5 minutes

Ingredients

- ¼ c. low-fat plain cream cheese
- 1 tbsp. raw honey
- 2 tsp. dark cocoa powder (70% cocoa or greater)
- 12 organic natural graham crackers
- 1 tbsp. raw cacao nibs

Instructions

1. Preheat broiler to high. Line a baking sheet with parchment paper.

2. In a small-sized mixing bowl, combine the cream cheese and honey; mix until smooth. Stir in the cocoa powder; mix until almost blended, leaving behind a few white and brown streaks for presentation.

3. Spread approx. 1½ tsp. of the cream cheese mixture onto each graham cracker. Arrange on baking sheet and transfer to broiler. Broil for 1 to 2 minutes, or until the mixture is soft and warm. Arrange crackers on serving tray and sprinkle each with cacao nibs. Divide crackers evenly and serve warm as either open-face or sandwiched together.

Mini Molten Chocolate Cakes W/ Hot Chocolate Sauce

Yield: 12 cakes
Servings: 6 (Serving Size: 2 cakes)
Total Time – Prep to Finish: 20 minutes

Ingredients

- 20 tablespoons (2½ sticks) butter
- 2 c. (16-oz) semisweet chocolate chips
- 1 c. all-purpose flour
- 3 c. confectioners' (powdered) sugar
- 6 large eggs
- 6 egg yolks
- 2 teaspoon vanilla extract
- 1 tsp. instant coffee powder (opt.)
- Powdered sugar for dusting (opt,)
- Fresh raspberries to garnish (opt.)
- (12) 6-ounce custard cups (ramekin cups) or
  cup muffin pan
- Nonstick cooking spray

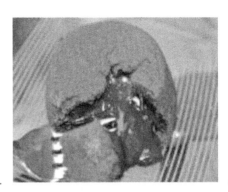

12-

Instructions

1. Preheat oven to 425° F. Spray each custard cup or the 12-cup muffin pan with non-stick cooking spray. In a medium-sized microwaveable mixing bowl, combine chocolate chips and butter. Place bowl in the microwave and heat for 60 at 50% power, then continue microwaving in 30-second intervals until butter and chocolate chips are completely melted and form a smooth and creamy consistency. Stir the flour and sugar into the chocolate-butter sauce and stir until fairly well blended.

2. Next, add the eggs and the egg yolks to the butter-chocolate mixture and stir with spoon or use an electric mixer until the ingredients are well blended. Next stir in the vanilla and instant coffee and stir until all ingredients are well combined.

3. Place an even amount of batter into each custard cup or muffin pan cup. If using custard cups, place the cups on top of a baking sheet. Place the baking sheet or muffin pan into the oven and bake for about 10 minutes or until the edges of each cake are firm but the center is runny. Run a knife around the edge to loosen and drop onto a serving dish. Dust each cake with powdered sugar and garnish with a couple fresh raspberries, if desired.

Coconut Macaroons Drizzled With Dark Chocolate

Yield: 16 macaroons
Servings: 8 (Serving Size: 2 macaroons)
Total Time – Prep to Finish: 30 minutes

Ingredients

- ½ c. sugar
- ¼ c. water
- ¼ c. coconut milk (full fat version)
- ¼ tsp. kosher salt
- 2 c. unsweetened desiccated coconut
- 1 egg white (approx. 3 tablespoons)
- ¼ c. dark chocolate chips
- ½ tsp. Fleur de Sel (opt.)

Instructions

1. Preheat oven to 350° F. Place a non-stick pan over medium heat; add in sugar, water, coconut milk, and salt. Bring to a medium simmer, and continue cooking an additional 5 minutes or until the mixture appears whitish in color, bubbly, and a little bit thinner than maple syrup but thicker than water.

2. Next, Place 1½ c. of flaked coconut in a medium-sized mixing bowl. Gradually stir the liquid sugar mixture into the coconut and stir until coconut is well coated. Now, stir in the egg white, then the remaining flaked coconut. Continue stirring until well mixed.

3. Using a small cookie scoop or ice cream scoop, pack the scoop firmly with the coconut mixture and place on a parchment paper-lined baking sheet. Place macaroons 2-inches apart. Place in oven and bake for 13 to 15 minutes or until the outer shell is golden brown and crispy to the touch. Remove baking sheet from oven, let macaroons cool on baking sheet for approx. 30 minutes. Meanwhile, prepare the dark chocolate drizzle by melting the chocolate chips in the microwave for 30 seconds and then in 15 second intervals, stirring in between intervals, until all chips are melted and the chocolate is smooth and runny enough to drizzle. Finally drizzle the dark chocolate over the tops of the macaroons and garnish each with a few sprinkles of Fleur de Sel (opt.)

Chocolate-Raspberry Brownies with Walnuts

Yield: 24 brownies
Servings: 12 (Serving Size: 2 brownies)
Total Time – Prep to Finish: 40 minutes

Ingredients

- 1/3 c. coconut flour
- 1/3 c. cacao powder
- 1/3 c. coconut butter or regular butter
- 5 eggs
- ½ c. agave syrup, of choice
- 2 tsp. vanilla extract
- ¼ c. walnuts, chopped
- ¼ c. frozen raspberries
- 2 tbsp. cacao nibs

Instructions

1. Preheat the oven to 350°F. Line a 9- x 9-inch baking dish with parchment paper.

2. In a large-sized mixing bowl, combine coconut flour and cacao powder. Mix well. Add in coconut butter, eggs, agave syrup, and vanilla extract. Using an electric hand mixer, beat the ingredients for about 2 minutes or until well blended.

3. Using a wooden spoon, fold in the walnuts, raspberries, and cacao nibs. Stir to incorporate.

4. Pour the mixture into the parchment-lined baking dish and place in preheated oven. Bake for 25 to 30 minutes or until a knife inserted in the middle comes out clean. Allow brownies to cool for 5 minutes in dish then cut into 1-inch squares. Serving size: 2 brownies.

Sliced Pears and Nut Butter Dip

Servings: 2
Total Time – Prep to Finish: 20 minutes

Ingredients:

- 1 c. almond butter or organic peanut butter
- 1/2 c. chunky, unsweetened applesauce
- 1/4 tsp. cinnamon
- 1-2 pears, sliced (enough to make 1 1/2 c. sliced pear)

Directions:

1. In a small mixing bowl, combine the almond butter (or organic peanut butter) and the apple sauce. Stir together until desired consistency is reached.

2. Wash and slice pear(s) so that you end up with 1½ c. of pear slices.

3. On two separate plates, divide the nut butter mixture and half of the mixture onto each plate.

4. Divide the pear slices into half and surround the nut butter with pear slices onto each plate. To garnish, sprinkle the nut butter (and pear slices, if desired) with 1/8 tsp. of cinnamon. Serve immediately.

Strawberry and Almonds Trail Mix

Yield: 2 servings
Total Time: 10 minutes

Ingredients:

- 1 c. almonds (raw or roasted)
- 1 c. pumpkin seeds
- 1/2 c. sunflower seeds
- 1 c. dried strawberries (or dried cranberries, if preferred)
- 1/2 c. raisins

Directions:

1. Using a seal-able plastic bowl, combine all ingredients into the bowl in the order listed. Seal the bowl with lid and toss to mix the ingredients well. Store in sealed bowl at room temperature for 2 weeks to 1 month.

Cocoa-Coconut Bites

Yield: 1 dozen bites
Servings: 3 (Serving Size: 4 bites)
Total Time – Prep to Finish: 10 minutes

Ingredients

- 1/2 c. almonds, raw or roasted
- 1/2 c. walnuts
- 1/2 c. pecan nuts
- 1/2 c. hazel nuts
- 1/2 c. pumpkin seeds
- 4 dates
- 3 to 4 tbsp. virgin coconut oil
- Unsweetened cocoa powder (begin with 3/4 tbsp., then to taste)
- 1/4 c. shredded coconut (begin with 1/4 c., then to taste)
- 1 c. shredded coconut

Directions

1. Place the 1 c. of shredded coconut into a shallow bowl and set aside.

2. Using s food processor, begin by grinding up all of the nuts and pumpkin seeds into as fine a floury powder as possible. Transfer the ground nut mixture to a bowl and set aside.

3. Now place the dates and shredded coconut into the food processor and grind until smooth. Remove the coconut mixture from the food processor and add to the bowl with the nut mixture. Blend the contents together thoroughly.

4. Next, mix in the cocoa powder beginning with 1/2 tbsp. and adding more if needed to taste. Finally stir in the coconut oil.

5. Once all the ingredients are blended together, begin rolling them into 1 1/2-inch balls and then roll each ball into the shredded coconut you had set aside earlier. Transfer the balls to the freezer and let them firm up for about 5 to 10 minutes. Place 4 balls on a plate and enjoy! Cocoa and Coconut Balls can be stored in seal-able container in the refrigerator for up to 2 weeks.

Roasted Rosemary Almonds

Yield: 1 cup
Servings: 4 (Serving Size: ¼ cup)
Total Time – Prep to Finish: 5 minutes

Ingredients

- 1 c. skin-on whole raw almonds
- 2 tbsp. dried rosemary
- 2 tsp. Kosher salt
- 1/4 tsp. fresh ground pepper
- 1 tbsp. butter

Directions

1. Place the almonds in a seal-able bowl. Set aside.

2. In a large non-stick skillet, melt the butter over medium-low heat. Once butter is completely melted and begins bubbling, pour in the almonds, taking care to keep them in a single layer, stirring constantly until the almonds are coated in the butter.

3. Once the almonds are coated, sprinkle in the rosemary, salt, and pepper. Stir and toss to mix the contents thoroughly.

Cranberry and Pumpkin Granola

Yield: 1 cup
Servings: 4 (Serving Size: ¼ cup)
Total Time – Prep to Finish: 10 minutes

Ingredients:

- 1 c. pecans, roughly chopped
- 1 c. walnuts, roughly chopped
- 1 c. unsweetened shredded coconut
- 1/2 c. pumpkin seeds (or sunflower seeds, if preferred)
- 1/4 c. sesame seeds
- 1/2 c. pumpkin puree
- 1/3 c. coconut oil
- 1/4 c. honey
- 2 tbsp. molasses
- 1 tbsp. vanilla extract
- 1 tbsp. + 1 tsp. ground cinnamon
- 1 tsp. nutmeg
- 1/4 tsp. ground cloves
- 1/4 tsp. sea salt
- 1 c. juice-sweetened dried cranberries (or raisins, if preferred)

Directions:

1. Preheat oven to 375°F. Line a baking sheet with unbleached parchment paper.
2. In a large mixing bowl, combine the pecans, walnuts, pumpkin seeds(or sunflower seeds), and sesame seeds. Divide the nut/seed mixture in half and place the first half in a food processor and process the mixture on high until the mixture finely chopped (you want to aim for a coarse-sand type of texture. Transfer the processed nut/seed mixture back to the large bowl and mix together with the remaining unprocessed half of the nut/seed mixture.
3. In a separate bowl, mix together the pumpkin puree, coconut oil, honey, molasses, vanilla extract, ground cinnamon, nutmeg, ground cloves, and sea salt. Stir to blend well. Pour this mixture over the nut/seed mixture and mix together until the nuts and seeds are completely coated.
4. Transfer the mixture onto the parchment-lined baking sheet, spread the granola evenly across the sheet. Bake in the preheated oven for 15 minutes, turning granola mixture over once halfway through baking time to prevent burning. Remove from the oven and let cool for about 5 minutes. Sprinkle dried cranberries (or raisins) over the top of the granola, then mix gently, right on the baking sheet. Place 1 c. into a sandwich bag or bowl and enjoy!

Raw Chocolate and Pumpkin Chia Pudding Parfait

Yield: 2 wraps
Servings: 2 (Serving Size: 1 wrap)
Total Time – Prep to Finish: 10 minutes

Ingredients

- 1 – 2 medium avocados to get1 c. avocado flesh, cut in chunks or slices.
- 1/2 c. soaked raw cashews (or you can process them in a food processor into a finely chopped powder-like consistency.
- 1/2 c. almond milk (or soy, coconut, or nonfat milk, if preferred)
- 1/2 c. pitted dates
- 1/4 c. plus ¼ c. pure maple syrup
- 1/3 c. raw cocoa powder
- 1/2 to 1 tsp. pure vanilla extract (or the seeds from one vanilla bean)
- 1/8 tsp. plus 1/8 tsp. sea salt
- 3/4 c. pure pumpkin (NOT pumpkin pie mix; try using the Farmer's Market brand at your local Farmer's Market - it's thick and organic)
- 3/4 c. plain or vanilla soy milk (may use coconut or almond milk)
- 1-2 tbsp coconut sugar (or a pinch stevia)
- 3 tbsp. white chia seeds (black will discolor pudding some)
- 1 tsp. cinnamon
- 1/4 tsp. freshly grated nutmeg
- 1/8 tsp. allspice
- pinch ground ginger (opt.)
- 1 tbsp. Dark Chocolate Shavings to garnish (opt)

Directions

1. First, prepare the chocolate mousse by placing into a blender, the chunks of avocado flesh, the soaked raw cashews (or finely chopped cashews), (or you can process them in a food processor into a finely chopped consistency), almond milk (or preferred), pitted dates, maple syrup, raw cocoa powder, first 1/2-1 tsp. pure vanilla extract (or vanilla bean seeds), and the sea salt.
2. Puree on medium-high speed for 1 to 2 minutes, or until smooth and there is no texture remaining from the cashews). Scrape down the sides of the blender and puree an additional 1 to 2 minutes. You want to reach a smooth, velvet-like pudding consistency.
3. Transfer blender contents to a bowl, cover and place in refrigerator. Wash out blender to use for next step.
4. Prepare the pumpkin chia pudding by placing into the blender the pure pumpkin, the plain or vanilla soy milk (or preferred), pure maple syrup, coconut sugar (or stevia), white chia seeds, cinnamon, freshly grated nutmeg, allspice, pinch of ground ginger (opt.), remaining sea salt, and remaining vanilla extract (or vanilla seeds from one bean).
5. Puree on medium-high for 1 to 2 minutes until the contents are smooth and well blended and thick. If you would like the pudding to be thicker, place in a bowl in the refrigerator for 20 minutes), add an additional tsp. of coconut sugar, or to taste, if you would like the pudding a bit sweeter.
6. Remove the chocolate mousse from the refrigerator. Divide the chocolate mousse pudding mixture among 2 parfait glasses. Now divide the pumpkin chia among and place half in each parfait glass. Garnish each parfait with a 1/2 tbsp. dark chocolate shavings, if desired. Serve immediately.

● ● ●

Carrot Sticks & Hummus

Yield: 2
Servings: 2
Total Time – Prep to Finish: 5 minutes

Ingredients

- 6 Carrot Sticks
- 1/2 c. Hummus

Directions

1. Serving size: 3 carrot sticks and 1/4 c. hummus – eat as a mid-morning snack
2. Can substitute the hummus for organic peanut butter or Nutella, if desired.

Fruit-Nut-Cheese Platter

Servings: 2
Total Time – Prep to Finish: 5 minutes

Ingredients

1. 1 to 2 apples, cored and cut into wedges – enough to make 1 c. of wedges
2. 1 large banana, sliced in half lengthwise, then sliced again to make 4 banana wedges
3. 2 to 4-ounces of cheddar cheese (or cheese of choice), cut into cubes or slices
4. 1/4 c. walnuts (or nuts of choice)

Directions

1. Prepare fruits and cheese as stated above.

2. On a plate, arrange 1/2 c. apple wedges, 2 banana wedges, 1 to 2-ounces cheddar cheese cubes or slices (or cheese of choice), and 1/8 c. walnuts (or nuts of choice).

3. Repeat process to make second serving. Serve immediately.

Mozzarella Cubes & Cherry Tomatoes

Yield: 2
Servings: 2 (Serving Size: 1oz. cheese, ½ c. tomatoes)
Total Time – Prep to Finish: 10 minutes

Ingredients

- 2 ounces of fresh Mozzarella, cut into cubes
- 1 c. cherry (or grape) tomatoes

Directions

1) Place 1-ounce of Mozzarella cubes onto a snack dish with 1/2 c. cherry (or grapes) tomatoes. Serve immediately.

Prosciutto & Dried Figs

Servings: 2 (Serving Size: 2 pcs. Prosciutto; 4 figs)
Total Time – Prep to Finish: 5 minutes

Ingredients

- 4 pieces (60 grams) Prosciutto
- 8 Dried Figs

Directions

1) On a small plate, place 2 pieces (approximately 30 grams) of prosciutto and 4 dried figs. Repeat with remaining ingredients for second plate. Serve immediately.

Vegetable Pesto Dip with Cucumber and Carrot

Yield: 1 cup dip
Servings: 2 (Serving Size: ½ c. dip)
Total Time – Prep to Finish: 10 minutes

Ingredients

- 1 c. freshly shelled English peas (or frozen peas, thawed)
- 2 cloves garlic, peeled and roughly chopped
- 1/4 c. grated Parmesan cheese
- 1/4 c. chopped fresh mint leaves
- Juice from one lemon
- 3 tbsp. extra virgin olive oil
- 2 tbsp. plus 1/4 c. of water, if necessary to thin
- Salt and pepper to taste
- 1 cucumber, sliced
- 1 c. carrot sticks

Directions

1. Place the peas, chopped garlic, parmesan cheese, chopped mint leaves, and lemon juice into a food processor and pulse until the mixture is slightly chopped. Scrape down the sides, and then pulse again.

2. Next, drizzle in the olive oil and blend on low speed for about 30 seconds or until smooth. Drizzle in 2 tbsp. of water, and continue to blend until smooth. Add additional water, up to 1/4 c., if needed to thin.

3. Add a pinch of sea salt and pepper, to taste and pulse until completely smooth. Taste to see if more salt and pepper is needed for seasoning. When preferred taste is reached, divide the pea pesto mixture in half and place each half into two dipping cups.

4. Serve the pesto with 1/4 to 1/2 c. sliced cucumber and 1/2 c. carrot sticks (or fresh vegetables of choice) for dipping. Serve immediately.

Strawberry Crunch Smoothie

Yield: 2 (8 oz.) smoothies
Servings: 2 (Serving Size: 1 (8 oz.) smoothie)
Total Time – Prep to Finish: 5 minutes

Ingredients

- 2 c. strawberries, frozen pref.
- 1 c. pineapple chunks, frozen pref.
- 1 c. low-fat vanilla soy-milk or skim milk
- 2 tbsp. frozen lemonade concentrate
- 1 c. low-fat vanilla yogurt
- 2 tbsp. honey (optional)
- 2 tbsp. chopped raw almonds

Directions

1. Place the strawberries and pineapple chunks in a blender.
2. Pour in soy milk or skim milk. Add the remaining ingredients, except for the honey.
3. Puree until smooth, pausing to push fruit into the blades of the blender, if necessary.
4. Add honey to blender, if desired, blend an additional 30 seconds.
5. Divide the smoothie mixture between two tall glasses. Garnish each smoothie with 1 tbsp. chopped almonds and drink immediately to receive full nutritional value.

Nut Butter Banana Wraps

Yield: 2 wraps
Servings: 2 (Serving Size: 1 wrap)
Total Time – Prep to Finish: 10 minutes

Ingredients

- 2 multigrain wraps
- 2 - 4 tsp. nut butter (of choice) or can use organic peanut butter instead)
- 1 banana, sliced (enough to make 1/2 c. of sliced banana)

Directions

1. Place 1 multigrain wrap onto each plate. Spread 1 to 2 tsp. nut butter (or organic peanut butter) onto the wraps.

2. Place 1/4 c. of banana slices onto each wrap and then roll the wraps up and serve immediately. Serving size equals one nut butter wrap.

Fruit Skewers

Yield: 6 skewers
Servings: 2 (Serving Size: 3 skewers)
Total Time – Prep to Finish: 15 minutes

Ingredients

- 1 to 2 c. watermelon, cubed
- 1 apple, cored and cut into wedges or cubes
- fresh strawberries, halved to make 1 to 1½ c.s
- 1 large banana, cut into 1-inch slices
- 1 c. mango, cut into chunks (opt.)
- 6 wooden skewers

Directions

1. Prepare fruits as directed above.
2. Take a skewer and begin threading on the fruit, in the order desired.
3. Place 3 fruit skewers per plate. Serving size = 3 skewers

Frozen Greek Yogurt

Yield: 6 cups
Servings: 12 (Serving Size: ½ c.)
Total Time – Prep to Finish: 45 minutes

Ingredients

- 2 c. plain whole-milk yogurt
- 2 c. plain nonfat or reduced-fat Greek yogurt
- 1/2 c. superfine sugar
- 3 tbsp. light corn syrup
- Fresh fruit or other toppings, for garnish

Directions

1. In a medium-sized mixing bowl, combine yogurts, sugar, and corn syrup. And whisk until well blended. Pour into ice cream maker and process according to manufacturer's instructions.

2. For a softer consistency, serve immediately. For a firmer consistency, place in a container with lid and freeze for up to 2 hours.

3. When ready to serve, garnish with toppings such as fresh fruits, granola, almonds, etc.

Apple Peanut Butter Bars

Yield: 10 bars
Servings: 10 (Serving Size: 1 bar)
Total Time – Prep to Finish: 30 minutes

Ingredients

- 2 c. rolled oats
- 1 c. shredded apple (one medium apple)
- ¼ c. peanut butter
- ½ c. honey
- 2 eggs
- ½ tsp. cinnamon
- ½ tsp. pure vanilla extract

Directions

1. Preheat oven to 350°F. Lightly grease a 9x9-inch baking dish and set aside.

2. Place all ingredients in an medium-sized mixing bowl and blend thoroughly.

3. Spread mixture into baking dish and use spatula to spread the mixture out, pressing the mixture down to spread across bottom of pan.

4. Place in preheated oven and bake for 18 to 20 minutes or until edges are lightly browned. Allow to cool before cutting into squares.

Made in the USA
Middletown, DE
20 July 2023

35491416R00091